THE
LOGIC OF
FORCE

A Fighter's View of Blunt-Force Encounters

This book is dedicated to Léroy Dinatale,
the oldest full-contact stick fighter on planet Earth.

THE
LOGIC OF
FORCE

A Fighter's View of Blunt-Force Encounters

JAMES LAFOND

TABLE OF CONTENTS

Chapter 1:   The Use of Force.. 1

Chapter 2:   The Basics of Brutality... 7

Chapter 3:   Balls in a Bottle: *Alcohol and Violence*......................... 13

Chapter 4:   Brains in a Ziploc Bag: *Drugs and Violence*................. 19

Chapter 5:   Life in the Missionary Position:
Clinches, Throws, and Floor Fights..................... 27

Chapter 6:   Upside Yo Head:
A Moment of Moral Silence for the Sucker Punch...........39

Chapter 7:   Shining Shoes: *Footwear as a Weapon*..........................41

Chapter 8:   Hitting That Messy Home Run: *Clubs*......................49

Chapter 9:   Walking Tall: *Sticks and Violence*........................... 61

Chapter 10:   Acting Small: *Rocks and Rocklike Weapons*................. 67

Chapter 11:   Utilize That Prehensile Thumb:
Improvised Weapons... 73

Chapter 12:   Crush! Kill! Destroy!
Tools, Vehicles, and Furniture as Weapons.....................81

Chapter 13:   On the Downside of Life:
Living Peacefully Amid Predation............................89

Chapter 14:   Beating the Odds:
A Summary of Relevant Findings.................. 91

"Those weapons which especially cause visible and invisible fractures, and bruise and crush in the bone out of its natural place, are rounded, smooth-surfaced, blunt, heavy, and hard. These bruise the scalp and pound it into a pulp."

—Hippocrates, *On Wounds in the Head*, ca. 400 B.C.

ACKNOWLEDGMENT

Thanks to Tattoo Rick and Jen for permitting me to use their bar as a research facility.

CHAPTER ONE

THE USE OF FORCE

> "Most animals on our world and theirs
> have a surrender reflex that prevents one
> member of a species from killing another.
> Humans use weapons instinctively. It
> makes the surrender reflex too slow."
> —Larry Niven and Jerry
> Pournelle, *The Mote in God's Eye*

According to conventional wisdom, we humans rose above the beasts in the field through our use of weapons. After conducting this study, I am not sure we rose above anything, other than what lies twitching at our feet.

For four years, I conducted an anecdotal and statistical study of violence in Baltimore, Maryland, as experienced by every person who was unlucky enough to make my acquaintance (however fleeting). This resulted in a survey of 1,675 acts of violence. (I know that the items below don't add up to 1,675, but some incidents are covered more than once. It is a miracle that the tally is only off by one.) In gross terms, the encounters broke down into four categories:

- 759 blunt-force assaults and armed fights
- 314 edged-weapons encounters
- 482 mass attacks, group fights, firearm encounters, and strangulations
- 121 mutual acts of unarmed combat or one-on-one fights

People in Baltimore City do not *fight* you; they *prey* on you.

Humans are social animals, and they therefore tend to attack one another in the most socially acceptable manner. The use of edged weapons and firearms brings down a lot of heat from the authorities, so we vicious apes tend to beat one another.

Let us review a few basic facts:

- Most uses of force are successful.
- Most uses of force go unpunished by the authorities.
- The most common use of force is blunt force.
- The most common type of weapon is a blunt weapon.
- Virtually all uses of blunt weapons go unpunished.

This book is simply a study of (1) all violence featuring the use

Above: The possible origin of the fist as a consequence of weapon use. Was the first punch thrown by a man who grabbed for a rock during a ground fight, with his hand closing on nothing and balling into a fist, who then struck a blow anyhow?

Right: Typical size disparity between antagonists.

of a blunt weapon and (2) all unarmed striking attacks, such as ambushes, sucker punches, and stompings.

One basic aspect of human-on-human violence is disparity of force. It is always present and usually favors the attacker. Whether an encounter is armed or unarmed, a mass attack or one-on-one, the typical size difference between antagonists is usually close to the male/female size gap for our species.

This book is primarily anecdotal, meaning it is about the stories of people caught in these types of violent situations. It is intended as a follow-up to *The Logic of Steel: A Fighter's View of Blade and Shank Encounters* (available as a PDF from Paladin Press). As a way of transitioning from that book to this one, for the first story I have chosen an example of an edged weapon being used in a manner more consistent with the use of blunt extension weapons.

PEELING DOUGH

Time of occurrence: night
Duration: seconds
Perspective: Big Gus, first-person defender

"This was the worse experience eva. Was out on the street—on the corna. Was a young dude, real tight; bodybuildin', wearin' tank top, headin' home. This dude, olda than me, talla, walks up with his hand down behind and says, 'Give me yo money, nigger.'

"I don't like that word, and I didn't see that he got anything, en I'm not given up ma money. I'm workin' stock at the time; humpin' freight for my cash—ain't given 'im shit. So I said, 'No,' and he swung this machete from behind—come overhead!

"I stepped back en put up the left arm, and it bit into the wrist. Cut me good through the outside, halfway in. I went down to the side from the force, en somebody was screamin'—a third party. So this dude runs, en still I got my cash. But I was pumpin' dark—not bright—blood into the street, losin' pressure. My skin was so tight at the time that it just peeled right back, as if you laid out some bread dough, sliced it with a knife, en peeled it back, just spreadin' open.

"Then this dude—a street thug like me, olda guy, not the kinda guy you expect to help—pulls up, takes off his shirt, wraps it around, and says, 'Apply pressure, and let me know if you start to pass out. No time ta wait for an ambulance; we gotta do it!'

"He got me in his ride and flew through red lights 'til he got me to the hospital. It took 13 stitches on the outside and 14 stitches on the inside. That was a close call. He keeps in touch en checks on how I'm doin'. He was the kinda guy you wouldn't expect to help no one. But he gave me the shirt off his back and saved my life."

FISH FOOD

Time of occurrence: day
Duration: under a minute
Perspective: The Mac Daddy, first-person aggressor

The following story is an example of an unarmed blunt force attack. It is categorized as an attack. However, if the aggressor had not attacked, it seems that the situation would have evolved into a group fight. This story does not strictly belong in this study, as it should be included in a mass attack study, but I can't pass up the opportunity to introduce The Mac Daddy, as he will be showing up throughout this book, and this was his favorite act of violence. The Mac Daddy is a friend of Big Gus, and they played on the same minor league football team together.

"I'm in the car as ma man's goin' inta the Chinese joint when these otha three dudes is comin' out. I'm five-eleven, three-hundred; he five-ten two-fitty. One a them little; two of em big bruthas—six-foot, two-fitty. One a them bumps en says, 'What up nigger?'

"Nasty, like that [the use of the N-word]. Ma man say, 'Who you callin' nigger, nigger?' while the two otha dudes comin' up behine. This all happen in the front doorway area of the Chinese joint, the carryout section. They didn't see me, didn't know I was there. He turns sideways and gives me the eye signal, and I know it's on.

"Now, The Mac Daddy normally cool, calm, collected—all 'bout love. We all bruthas—even you—in the eye of the Lord. But when it come time to throw down—ta back up a brutha—The Mac Daddy become a chump-crushin' machine! It the fear. You don' wan me ta fear ya; that when the anga come—especially when that word [the

N-word] is used nastily. When The Mac Daddy become angray, he get the urge ta break ribs en jaws, ta hear the crack a the bones!

"Now, that not the preferred Mac Daddy persona. I don' wan' the anga en the violence. That why I practice negotiatin'. But den you got some unreasonable dudes . . .

"I walk in like I'm a customer. I knew it was ready time as soon as I heard the conversation. As I headed in, I punched this one big dude in the back of the head, right in the side of his ear from behind. He go forward, and ma man is on the otha big dude, crackin' him to the floor.

"Now this little one standin' in front a me, he was lookin' this way for an escape, look at me, look that way for an escape, look at me—en I punch 'im in the jaw twice jus' for bein' there. He go down. No gettin' up for him.

"Meanwhile ma man is punishin' this dude for callin' him a nigger, stompin' a mudhole in 'is ass—wearin' his ass out. The fist dude comin' to his feet about now, on hands 'n knees, crawlin' toward this giant fish tank these Chinese people have across the front wall, with these big culaful fish. He was gettin' up, becomin' a threat. So I grabbed 'im by the back of 'is shirt and shoved 'im. He put out his hand to stop 'iself, and it went through the middle of the glass. His head hit the corna of the tank, and the whole thing cracked.

"The police had been called already—kinda early, I thought. You could hear the sirens, and all these tiny Chinese people were running around chattering—they couldn't speak much English. The lady though, she was yellin', 'You get out!'

"I said, 'Come on, Yo,' to ma man. But he was still stompin' that dude, en I had ta pull 'im off. We hauled ass! You don' wanna escape inna car cause someone'll get a tag number, en the police git ya later on. They hadn't seen us drive up or get out of the car. So we ran to our buddy's house around the corna.

"When this buddy walked up later to get the car, he talked to some people while all the cops and the ambulances was there. The two big dudes was on stretchas. The Chinese people couldn't give a good description, but one customa was tryin'. You know how some people say some otha people all look the same? So what do the police got? Two big bruthas beatin' down two big bruthas—happens all the time."

CHAPTER TWO

THE BASICS OF BRUTALITY

The violent encounters described in this book took place largely in Baltimore City, often in the shadows of abandoned factories, boarded-up residential areas (there are approximately 20,000 vacant homes in Baltimore), and deserted retail districts. The perpetrators were generally poorly educated human beings but highly educated predatory primates.

If you are considering this subject from a self-defense point of view, then you definitely want to focus on avoiding such situations through tactical awareness. Even then, if you end up in the dangerous situation, you should attempt to defuse it verbally or with body language. If that fails, then do whatever you can to remain a threat. Remember, this is not a fight. You cannot tap . . . well, you can.

Once you have been physically compromised, your attacker can carry out his master plan, which has nothing to do with victory. That plan is to hurt, maim, or kill you.

The fight, if there is one, is just a means to an end. Anybody can finish a downed opponent, provided he has the stomach for it, and your attacker has already proven he's got the appetite.

Doing your fellow man in once he has been physically compromised is not really any more difficult than eating shellfish—a pointed or blunt object may help, but, hell, otters and raccoons make out just fine. Then there are the legal ramifications of any attack you do succeed in defeating.

This all suggests the importance of avoidance. Permit me to illustrate some antiviolence techniques in the story below, in which I was a participant.

V8 SUM-BITCH

Chuck and I stepped into a South Baltimore bar in the middle of the block on a residential side street at 6:00 A.M. to shoot pool after work one winter morning. I stepped up to the bar next to a large, hairy man who was drinking draft; ordered the ingredients for my virgin mary; and mixed it on the bar next to him. He growled in an emasculating tone, "You forgot the Worcestershire sauce, pal."

I slapped him on the shoulder as I headed back to the table and said, "Only pussies drink their tomato juice with Worcestershire sauce."

After choking on his beer, the brute laughed and said, "You're all right, man," and followed me back to the table, where he introduced himself.

"Name's Harvey, worked on snow removal for two days en been workin' on drinkin' ma pay since yesterday mornin'—got 16 bucks left outta two beans. Down ta drinkin' draft. How 'bout I play y'all fer rounds?"

Now, every guy who grew up in that neighborhood grew up in a barroom shooting pool. I sucked, and Harvey played in a league. This was tantamount to telling me that I would be paying for his drinks. That is, this would have been the case *if* not for the 60 or so bottles of beer Harvey had consumed over the preceding 24 hours. He kept scratching on the eight-ball as Chuck tried not to snicker at the huge man.

The conversation turned to upbringing, occupation, and age. Both Harvey and I were 36 (he showed me his driver's license). When I became the first man in some months to defeat Harvey in eight-ball despite my obvious lack of skill, he said, "You V8 sum-bitch, it's that juice—it had to be, or you're damn lucky."

I handed Harvey my expired learner's permit. A dark cloud of superstition clouded his eyes as he knitted his hairy brows and said, "Goddamn, we got the same birthday. You got ma number! Where you live?"

"In the Northeast" [on the other side of a 5-mile-deep black ghetto].

"That's a dangerous area. You can't drive on this permit. How you get here at night?"

Chuck blurted, "He takes the dang bus, if you can believe that!"

As Harvey stood in awe, I handed him a "Violence Guy" business card. "I find my status as an honorary African-American enables me to access normally untapped sources for my study."

Harvey was such a racist that he was incredulous about my claim to have interviewed black men on their own turf.

"Ya mean you talk to the homeboys, like you're Doctor Dolittle?" [This is possibly the most racist statement I have ever recorded.]

Chuck interjected, "Not only can he understand what they say, some a the big scary ones even call him 'ma brutha.' I've seen it!"

Harvey looked at my scrawny little person sheepishly with glazed eyes and declared, "You one of them stone-cold hillbilly killers—the story-tellin' kind, like a sorcerer."

From that point on, as far as Harvey was concerned, I was some righteous, white-trash, special-ops race-warrior with a mythic edge. I then spent an hour interrogating him about the details of his violent, alcohol-sodden life. He showed me great respect and refused to sit in my presence.

What underlined Harvey's superstitions concerning me was a rather simple equation. When I walked in, Harvey just saw me as potential prey. I was not large enough to be a credible opponent; I was too different to bond with and too arrogant to ignore. Even Harvey, though drunk and no doubt the victor in whatever brawl might have ensued between us, had his eye out for the face-saving device. For him it was my bizarre lifestyle and the fact that I routinely went alone where he was afraid to go, into the enclaves of his lifelong enemies. Harvey chose the enemy-of-my-enemy route to peace among men.

• • •

Barroom situations in isolated urban enclaves can be very dicey, as the patrons of these local dives often have the same xenophobic mindset as a medieval villager. Verbal solutions to avoiding and suppressing violence are most effective indoors. Body language, awareness, and other tactical considerations (such as your pace, route,

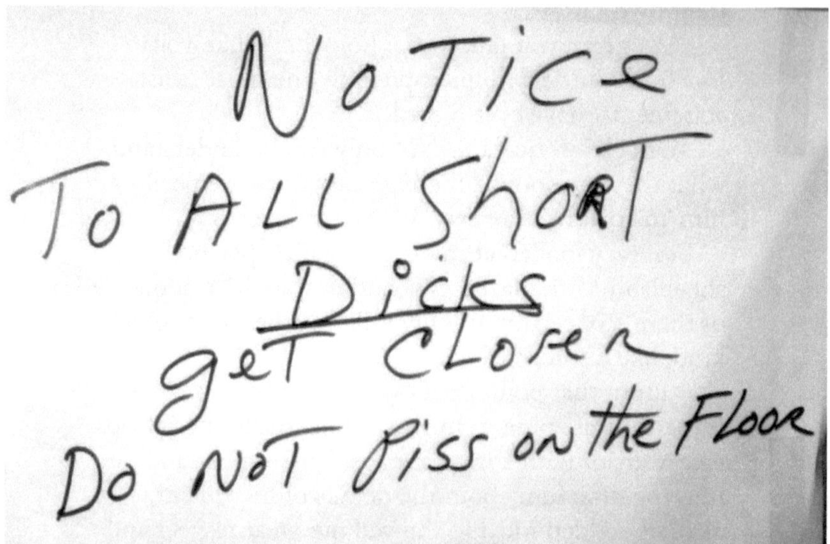

A sign in the men's room at the bar where I met Harvey.

A bar in one of the black areas of Northeast Baltimore. The bartender hands out 40s of malt liquor from behind a bulletproof cage, and the patrons stand on a concrete slab. Broken furniture is piled in a corner of the one-room establishment.

A Northeast Baltimore bar where I conducted many of the interviews for this book.

attire, potential weapons, and comments, as well as the controlling distance between you and others) count for a lot more out in the sterile wilderness between buildings.

CHAPTER THREE

BALLS IN A BOTTLE

Alcohol and Violence

"Since he [Cole Younger] believed that the Northfield raid had been botched because the three gang members who went into the bank were drunk, he became a fierce temperance advocate."
—Edward E. Leslie, *The Devil Knows How to Ride*

Welcome to the low IQ-alcohol-violence love triangle. One cold winter night I was interviewing Davy, a meth distributor who brought product in from Philly and Delaware and had local wholesalers funnel it to the actual dealers. Davy did not use drugs, but he drank a lot. This particular night he was having a crisis of faith. He claimed to be a devout Catholic, and when his big, beefy hand covered mine and put my pen in his pocket, I knew he was about to come clean.

It turns out that Davy had just recently beaten, tortured, and threatened one of his wholesalers who was behind on payments. He did not have a problem with breaking into the guy's house and terrorizing him, but he was ridden with guilt over the fact that he had killed the man's rottweiler. The death of the dog haunted him.

"I was so mad at that prick for making me kill his dog that I almost killed him. That was a good dog just doing its job. And I had to kill it with my own hands."

Just then we were rudely interrupted by a tall, skinny, and extremely drunk redneck, who was pawing all over the only good-looking woman in the place, who happened to be sitting next to

Davy. The drunk scolded Davy for talking while the band played, telling him that he had no class. A few verbal exchanges ensued as Davy, the bartender, and I alternately threatened the guy. He eventually left the bar and ran straight into four coked-up football players who had just come back from a drug run downtown. When the drunk redneck called them "pussies," he was beaten, stomped, and left in the center of the street.

Such are the "opponents" that pad the records of champion "bar fighters." Jerks with low alcohol tolerance or who grow beer balls enjoy a symbiotic relationship of sorts with violent, functional alcoholics. I did end up classifying the righteous stomping of the redneck by the cokeheads as an attack. It was not a mutual combat by any stretch—just baboon-level justice.

One of the few things that keeps drunks from fighting constantly in public is the threat of armed retaliation. The most violent places on earth are certain working-class bars in England that are so rough that some bouncers have attained the status of champion athletes.

One example of the other extreme was the old Eldorado Lounge in Baltimore. When you stepped through the door, Chico, a heavyweight boxer, would pat you down for weapons. The establishment was 10 feet wide and 90 feet long, most of it occupied by a bar and the stage—a bright-white ecosystem supporting five nude Afro-Asian vixens and maintained by three tuxedoed mixologists. Perhaps 200 black men decked out in shades, chains, and up-to-date athletic wear, flashing thick knot-rolls of cash, patronized the place.

The Eldorado might be a model of tolerance and nonaggression now, but Chico told me that it had not always been so peaceful. As soon as he instituted the pat-downs at the door, though, the fights ended. The unspoken point was that nobody wanted to roll the dice on whom Chico would toss out first, because if you were second to hit the pavement, your opponent would be that much closer than you to his Saab or BMW, and hence the comfort and solace of his 9mm handgun.

When violence does erupt during the partaking of alcohol, there is no shortage of makeshift blunt weapons available. What's better, since most of these weapons are glass, is that if they break you're in possession of an edged weapon.

Using a beer mug to blind, jab, or hammer an opponent.

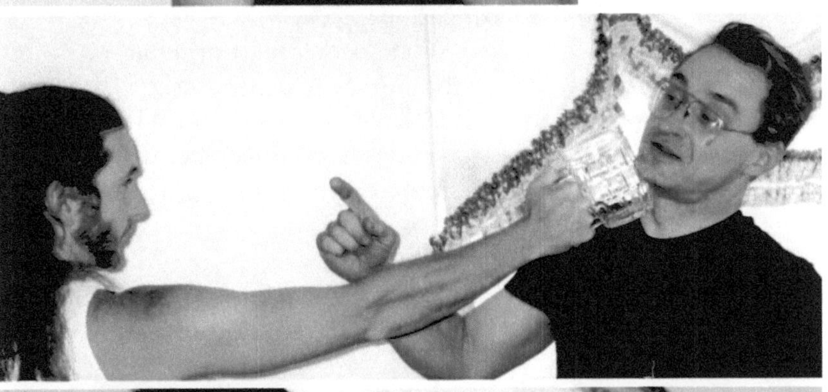

ADVICE FROM BARTENDERS ON HANDLING DRUNKS

"You can't talk to a drunk. It almost always makes him worse. Ignore him, leave, call the police, or find someone to kick his ass!"

—Pepper

"I've been behind this bar since I was 17. It's my job to nip any problem in the bud. The job of a good bartender is to tell customers when they've had enough. For the most part, people who stay with beer are fairly mellow. When people start drinking the hard shit, you see the animal. Mixing whiskey with beer is trouble. Whiskey is an accelerator. The sad part is that the worst ones won't remember what they did the next day, so there's no learning process or self-regulation."

—Massy

"Fucking kick their head in and drag them 50 feet from the establishment."

—Tattoo Rick

"I can kick his stupid ass to begin with. What's he gonna do when he's so drunk he can't walk straight? All I have to do is remind the fool what's gonna happen if he keeps up with the nonsense. That whiskey grows two big balls but takes away what ya need ta back 'em up."

—Sand Man

CONFESSIONS ABOUT
ALCOHOL ABUSE

"Drinkin' this shit brings out the beast. I'm a jerk
when I'm drunk. I've been barred from every bar in
Highlandtown and Greek Town. Being loud, brave,
and stupid all at once really changes the way people
treat you. Fuck 'em."

—Daniel

"I'd start out drinking at the upscale end of
town with a client. A few hours later he's home with
the wife, and I'm drinking with some working guys
at a decent blue-collar bar. By the wee hours of the
morning, I'm drinking next to a broken-down slob
propped up in the corner of a bar in East Baltimore.
We might be the only ones there. But as long as he's
there, I'm still not a drunk, because I can point to
him and say, 'Now that's a drunk.' When you drink
that way, you always want to drink where you feel
superior. I thought I was having a great time until
the judge told me what I was."

—Ted

"I only drink under certain social conditions, like
with my school buddies at the Country Music Jam-
boree, where a certain amount of rowdiness is toler-
ated and I have friends capable of restraining me in
case things get crazy. My tendency to become hateful
when drunk is bothersome, so I drink infrequently.
My involvement in the combat arts is, I think, part
of this need to maintain self-control, especially since
I have a family."

—Dan

THE CIRCLE

Time of occurrence: day
Duration: under a minute
Perspective: eyewitness

At the Circle Bar & Grill, two young men argued over a girl. One pulled a bat from his car and took a swing at the other, who ducked, resulting in the bat striking and denting a car driven by a group of six men. The men swarmed the batter, disarmed him, shoved him to the ground, and stomped him for about 30 seconds. The witness took the injured batter to the hospital.

DUKE

Time of occurrence: night
Duration: under 10 seconds
Perspective: first-person defender

Duke was working the door at a big club in Texas when "a punk muthafuca" began hassling one of the waitresses at a table. Duke walked over, leaned on the table, and "asked the boy ta leave."

The punk picked up a beer glass and swung it overhand, striking Duke across the bridge of the nose with the bottom. Duke's nose exploded, spurting blood from both nostrils. As Duke lunged for the now fleeing punk, the waitress stepped in front of Duke and held a napkin to his nose. By the time he made it to the front door with the bloody napkin pressed to his nose, the punk was pulling out of the parking lot.

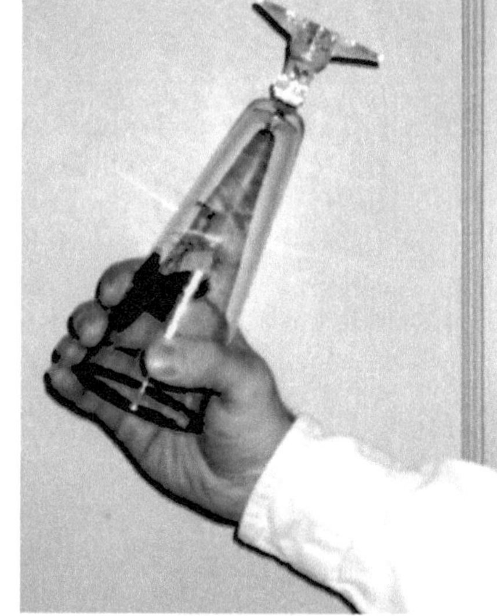

The beer glass wielded as a weapon.

BRAINS IN A ZIPLOC BAG

Drugs and Violence

One hot June night as I waited for the #19 bus on Harford Road, I was approached by a young man who shouted, "Yo, yo got money?"

I snarled, shifted my weight, and looked side to side, keeping him in my field of vision. He backed off, and I boarded.

After I got off the bus at the Inner Harbor, I walked through Federal Hill and South Baltimore, infested with crackheads, meth-heads, cokeheads, and heroin addicts. Panhandling is often used as a pretext for attacks in this area. While I was crossing Fort Avenue, two construction workers in a blue pickup truck screamed, "Queer!" and swerved toward me as they drank from bottles of beer.

After my shift the next morning as I stepped off the bus on Harford and Southern across the street from a rehab clinic, I passed a young man who made hard eye contact with me. He scanned my hands and belt line. Since I was getting off an out-of-town bus with work gear on a Saturday morning, he reasoned that I would be carrying cash. When he tried to make eye contact with me again, I read this as an attempt to initiate a confrontation. I declined, looked around for possible accomplices, and walked past him.

As I passed, he rose and turned to follow me up Southern Avenue. Deciding to stab him, I shifted my gear into my left hand so that I could draw the screwdriver from the sleeve of the leather kneepads I carried. When I stopped and stared at him, he stopped advancing, stepped back against the light pole, and slumped back down to the ground.

These passing encounters marked a rather typical weekend for me at that time (late 1990s), living in that neighborhood and working that job. From 2006 through 2010 working as general manager of a supermarket in a drug-infested area of Northeast Baltimore, I would log up to 20 confrontations per week with panhandling dope fiends on the front sidewalk and parking lot, while my 260-pound security man sat in the office watching live video of some cashier's big butt. After years of avoiding confrontations, I had to initiate them as part of my job. Then, after eight hours of aggressive policing in a tie, I'd throw the choker in a locker, slap on a rag and jacket, and become a defender again back at the bus stop.

My two favorite freaks were Blond Boy, a sore-covered heroin addict who was built like mixed martial arts (MMA) fighter Tyson Griffin, and Keith of the much-pierced face, who was also blond but taller. One evening an irate woman who claimed she had been panhandled by Blond Boy called me to the front of the grocery store. I ran outside, knowing he would still be scavenging for goodwill. He had an older lady pinned in her car and was screaming that he needed money. (I think, at this time, my security man was zooming in on Tannika's ample cleavage.) Retail food geek in a tie to the rescue!

I ran up to within five paces of Blond Boy and stopped. He then turned dramatically, with his hands on the side of his head, his face turning purple, and screamed, "You, you! You are such an *asshole!*"

I replied, "Yes, that's my job. You have to leave."

He responded, "Why do you have to be such an *asshole?!* I'm sick of you bothering me. Stay away. I'm known for knocking people out!"

"Good, we ought to get along just fine," I replied, "because I'm known for taking beatings. Come on back to the bus stop and knock me out tonight. But right now, you need to leave."

At this point his mind began processing some violent threat or action but was short-circuited by the customer who had complained about him. She had her right arm around my waist and was screaming over my right shoulder while she aimed a container of Mace over my left shoulder, all the while pressing her hard nipples into my back. She was screaming at Blond Boy, "Die, mutherfucker. Starve in a gutter! I'll fuckin' Mace your ass."

Luckily for me she did not spray the Mace, and Blond Boy fled in fear of this little blonde who got her rocks off threatening dope fiends with Mace. I then assisted the elderly woman from her car while the psychotic—but actually hot—white-trash vixen waited. She told me she liked Italian food, was a single mother, wanted me to beat up her brother, and . . . somehow I lost interest.

The really great part about this incident was that, when I informed the police that I was becoming tired of Blond Boy, they went after him—and got Keith instead. Now Keith and Blond Boy are two of only three blond men in Baltimore City, so we can forgive the cops. Keith resisted arrest, and the cops stomped him out in front of the gay bar down the street.

About three months later, Keith came to the storefront and paced back and forth on the sidewalk. Apparently, my security man had grown bored waiting for the last button on Ashantai's long-suffering, undersized blouse to pop and had done a perimeter walk. He came to me, about ready to have an asthma attack, and begged, "Boss, this bad white boy outside, could you please ask him to go?"

I went outside and dazzled Keith with my eloquence and diction. I think I even called him sir. Keith had been looking to throw down with me, but upon seeing my sweating and heavily breathing security man behind me (*way behind me*), he apparently mistook the adrenaline dump gone bad as the eagerness of a predatory homosexual and decided to leave.

I could go on and on about imposing my will on dope fiends without actually having to touch them. It really is a nonphysical art. Out of a probable 1,200 panhandler ejections over a four-year period, I only had to fight with one, and that was over with a single headbutt between his eyes.

But still, even after my stint at the Ghetto Grocery Store as the crappiest bouncer in Baltimore, every time I am approached by some parasite who wants me to finance his peculiar form of suicide, a debate rages within me between my brain and my guts. Should I walk around or stand my ground?

Let's take a look at how some others have handled the dope fiends of Baltimore.

IRENE AND THE REPROBATE

Time of occurrence: night
Duration: under 10 seconds
Perspective: Irene, first-person defender

"I was coming home from work—waiting for the bus—when this homeless man approached me and asked for a cigarette. I didn't have a cigarette, so he cussed me. He had a reprobated mind. I didn't have a weapon, so I got up and left. If I hadn't, there would have been an altercation."

DEE AND THE DOPE FIEND

Time of occurrence: night
Duration: minute plus
Perspective: Dee, first-person aggressor

"This gentleman had been pushing a shopping cart with his lady, who had walked out with a loaded backpack. When he came through without a purchase but with a loaded backpack, I approached him respectfully and told him he wasn't leaving with that heavy backpack.

"He was tall and darn near 40. But he was two feet taller than I am, and he didn't want to go down. I tackled him in the deodorant aisle, and we plowed into the shelf. He wasn't actually trying to hurt me; he just wanted to break free. But I finally got him cuffed.

"The police were there within 10 minutes, but they wouldn't take him in. He had $86 worth of candy in that bag, and we could write him up for the damaged deodorants. But because he had a valid Maryland ID and hadn't taken $300 worth of product, he just got a citation.

"I treat shoplifters with respect. They don't get locked up—I mean how is a guy going to run out of a market with $300 worth of food? This guy had a drug problem—he had needles in his pockets. It is important that they look at you as a guy who is just doing his job. You don't want somebody coming back to take a shot at you."

YEBITS AND THE NARC HUNTER

Time of occurrence: night
Duration: minutes
Perspective: Yebits, first-person defender

"I was sitting in this dark girlie bar with my buddy, when this small guy sat up next to me on my right side and said, 'How does it feel to bust someone and put 'em in jail?'

"'Sorry, I don't know what you're talking about,' I responded.

"'You're a fuckin' narc. You busted my brother.'

"'Look, I work for Gunman Aircraft; here's my ID. I'm no narc.'

"He wouldn't let up. 'Now we're going to take care of this nice and quiet,' he said as he put this knife to my side. It was a big sheath knife, and he was holding it in his left hand. He was looped.

"I turned to my buddy (sitting to my left) and said, 'He's got a knife.'

"My buddy got hold of the bartender, who put a .38 in this guy's face, took the knife, and said, 'Get out.'

"A few minutes later the guy came back in with another knife, a

A haven for dope fiends and hard-core alcoholics, this unsavory den is located a mere hundred yards from major tourist and entertainment attractions. By day it's deserted; by night it's a center for prostitution.

smaller sheath knife, and held it to my side. I made my move, grabbed his wrist with both hands, and yelled, 'He's got a knife! Get the knife!'

"Bouncers came over just as we were going down, and they took him down and lumped him up a bit. Got my licks in too. We took him out on the lot and made him leave. He's getting in his Ford LTD, and we're banging on his car saying, 'Get out of here, you crazy SOB!'

"He floored it into reverse out into Route 40 and hit this guy broadside—folded the car right in half—got caught up, floored it, and dragged the guy with him as he's trying to break free. He breaks free, and the other guy is chasing him down Route 40. I don't know how the guy could drive the way he had been hit. The whole thing was insane."

AN EAR FOR AN INCH

Time of occurrence: night
Duration: minutes
Perspective: Duncan, first person

Duncan was highly intelligent, stood 6 foot 4, weighed in at 240, had piercing—almost possessed—eyes, and a black beard that grew nearly up to his eyes. He could definitely play the heavy in a Rob Zombie film.

"I like violence. It's fun and is usually over before you're tired. This is my favorite.

"I was young, perhaps 30, and bouncing at this bar. It was pretty crowded, and this PCP freak—a short, stocky guy—started with this chick and punched her in the jaw. By the time I got across the room, he had punched the girl's boyfriend and the owner.

"I put him in a full nelson, walked him over to the door, and opened it with his face. Then somebody pushed me out the door. I turned around, and this guy's friend was coming out behind me, unhitching his chain belt. I was between these two, deciding who I was going to kill first, and my friend—who is a lot bigger than I am and just happened to be riding by—stopped his car in the middle of the street and got out. He basically disposed of the twerp with the chain. I don't know what he did because I was busy with the freak.

"As this guy rushed me, I punched him in the face, grabbed him, picked him up, slammed him, and kicked him in the face with the toe of my shoe. I also kicked him when he was getting up to charge me again. He kept getting up and charging me. He obviously wasn't feeling a thing. This sequence was repeated numerous but uncounted times.

"I started to get tired, so I got low with a [shoulder] butt, putting it into his chest for a scoop. I felt something and looked down, and this freak was biting me, trying to tear off a piece. [The resulting sunken scar on Duncan's left shoulder is the size of a silver dollar.]

"I'm thinking, *What the fuck is this? Well, two people can play that game, pal.* This guy was munching away, so I decided that I was going to take something from him too. I looked [down] over my shoulder, and all I saw was this ear. So I bit it and ripped it off. It stayed in my mouth—I didn't spit it out.

"The cops pulled up, saw the blood, and took us to the hospital, with the girl he had punched. I wasn't hurt, but there was blood everywhere. The funniest thing was the ear. It was stuck between my teeth, and I couldn't get it out. I wiggled it and worked it but couldn't pull it loose until we got to the hospital. I was treated and released. Of course, the girl was there, and she was real happy with me—*real grateful.*

"I was later charged with maiming and disfiguring. I didn't know there was even a law for that. I found out that I was facing 20 years. When I got into court and saw that the judge was a lady, I thought it was all over.

"The guy who lost the ear—a real dirtbag—said his piece, and then it was my turn. I had witnesses, and I told the judge that I had been working as a bouncer and this guy was hitting patrons and employees. When I ejected him, he wanted to fight and took the first bite. I said, 'Your honor, an eye for and eye, a tooth for a tooth. Just like the Bible says, hon.'

"She was getting sick. She threw up her hands and said, 'This is disgusting. Everybody just get out of my courtroom.'

"She threw it out. I beat the rap, and I had been sweating it too. Overall, I would have to say it was a positive experience: I had a great fight, got paid, got laid, got a souvenir, and beat the charges. What's not to like?

"I kept the ear. It was about half an ear—a lot more than Tyson got! I put it in a baby food jar and kept it on the back of the kitchen sink for about a year. Eventually it got really funky, so I threw it out.

"A couple of years later I met this nice older guy and he said, 'You probably know my son. You're about his age.' It was the guy's dad. I said, 'Yeah, probably.'

"I didn't have the heart to tell him how well we were acquainted."

CHAPTER FIVE

LIFE IN THE MISSIONARY POSITION

Clinches, Throws, and Floor Fights

Although fans of MMA, including me, have come to identify grappling as a tactical measure used to nullify an opponent's advantage in striking, criminal attackers grapple primarily to smash the victim's head into a hard chunk of the environment, such as a wall, automobile, or sidewalk, or to put him in a position where he can be robbed, raped, or stomped. This mentality is purely predatory and does not really have a counterpart in sports competition.

Below are a series of real grappling stories and a number of photo reconstructions of signature grappling tactics used by some of the subjects of this study. Remember, this type of grappling is often about the application of lethal doses of blunt force. The first story dovetails nicely with the subject matter of the previous chapter.

LIL' BERRY

**Time of occurrence: night
Duration: various lengths
Perspective: Lil' Berry, first-person aggressor**

"I was dealin' outta my house in Hamden—had the keys [kilos of cocaine] delivered to the house. Used to cut it right there in the living room. Got to be a real hassle: junkies coming to the house; people not payin'; worryin' 'bout narcs—you know, a pain in the ass. So I drank a lot.

"I got in a fight with this junkie over somethin' stupid—right on the living room floor. I was really pounding him [from the mount], so my girl tried to break it up. Now, she was the type of girl who would fight, would help you in a fight. So this other junkie—the junkie's buddy—thought it was a pile-on situation, and grabbed her; and it cooled down.

"Then she told me he grabbed her tits. So I was like, 'Oh really? This is nice. Here we go again.' So I put on my brass knuckles—they had spikes like daggers—and got on top of him, punching holes in his face. He was really messed up, in a coma for three weeks. I was charged with attempted murder, but I paid off his family—gave them a few grand—and I ended up getting off.

"Last night, the cops flyin' down Fort [Avenue] to Light [Street]; they were comin' for me. I'd been living with the homeless up in Frederick [Central Maryland] for the past three years, and I decided ta come back to Baltimore and get a job. So I stopped at my mom's house. I walked in and asked, 'What the fuck is up?'

"My brother said, 'My kid is sleepin' upstairs; watch your language,' real disrespectful like.

"Well, he's a crackhead and he owes me money, and I'm drunk, so we went at it. He nailed me in the eye with a right cross, and I kicked him in the stomach [with a foot jab]. He grabbed me and rocked me pretty good with another cross, and I pulled him down on top of me.

"Mom got down in between us, and we didn't wanna hit her— she's Mom! So we stopped.

"Five-O showed up, and I talked to them and had to go. But I went around back, snuck in, and came up behind that prick and put him in a sentry choke. Then I beat the side of his head in with these three mashed knuckles—got my money back, homeboy."

Now, is there any doubt in your mind that Lil' Berry would bite your nose off in a floor fight?

BIG LARRY

Time of occurrence: night/day
Duration: under a minute
Perspective: first-person aggressor

"I was working security at the Stop, Shop, & Save in Waverly. I'm 6-3, 314. Was workin' with a big, young, muscular boy—a veteran. We stopped this shoplifter. I came up to his shoulder, and he was much wider than me. Did not want to cooperate. Started punching at us, so I got in behind him and put on a full nelson. When his arms went up, this machete fell out from under his coat. I kicked it over to the manager and told him to put it in the office. My partner goes under him from the front, and we took him down.

"The police were all responding—females and everything. When they start to fight you, the 911 call goes out, and the officers are good to respond."

"DON'T SAY IT LIKE YOU FROM MISSISSIPPI"

Time of occurrence: night
Duration: seconds
Perspective: The Mac Daddy, first-person aggressor

"This was outside a club, started by a chump. The Mac Daddy don' have no wrong intentions. [Yes, the inevitable protestation of innocence!] I'm walkin' up en this dude lookin' at me like he know me—shouldn' be lookin' like that at someone he ain't tight with. So I say, 'What you lookin' at? What's yo problem?'

"He say, 'What you lookin' at, nigger?'

"Said it like that, like we in Mississippi—real nasty like. I said, 'Who you callin' nigger?'

The lineup is favored by untrained punchers against smaller adversaries.

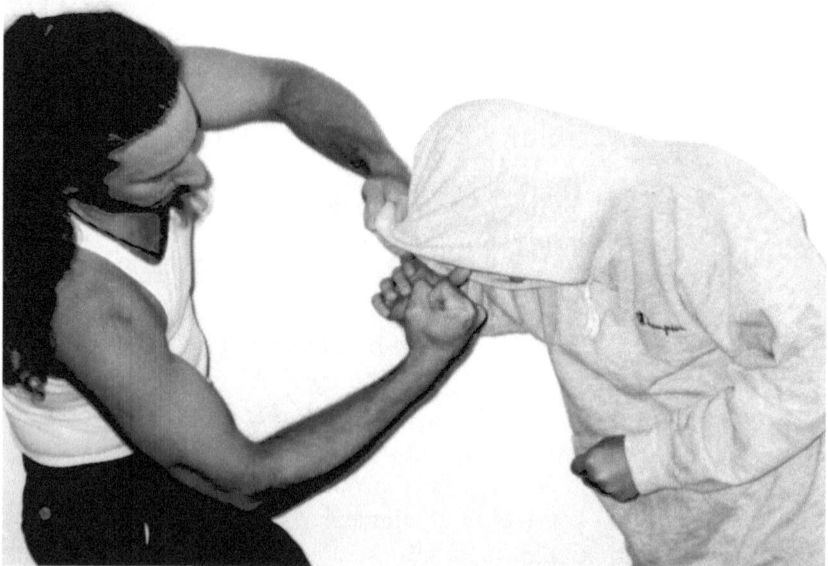

The hoodie is used for pulling a shorter man into an uppercut.

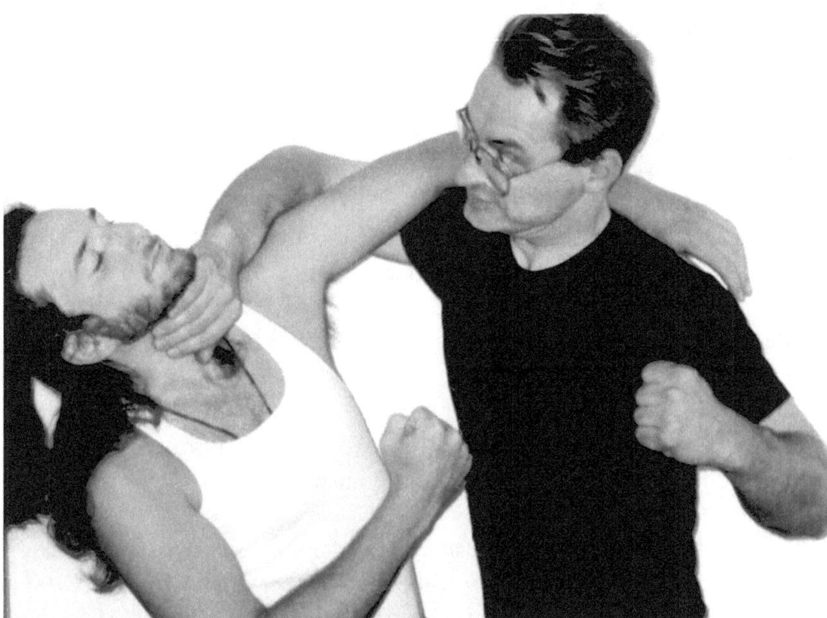

Duncan's crank is a counter to an overextended left hook.

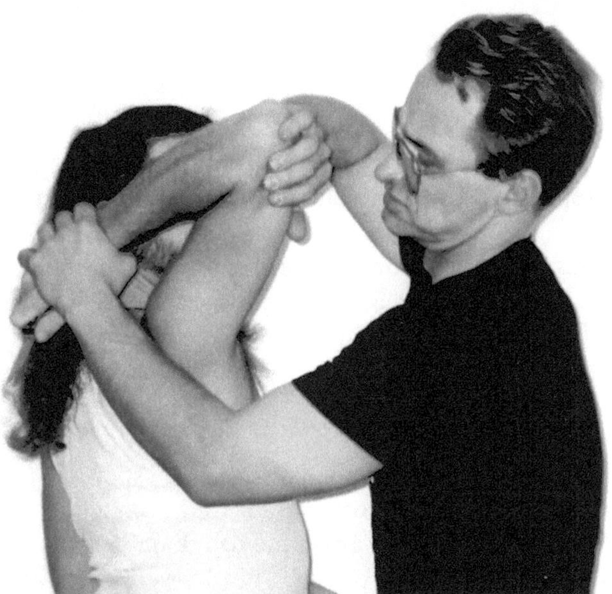

Duncan's shoulder crank.

"His friend, he was with was my friend, and his friend says to this chump, 'If you start trouble, you on your own.'

"Now he 'bout my height, but only 170 to my 270. He cornaback size. I was offensive tackle—eat them boys fo' lunch. Loved runnin' sweeps right ova they little asses—crunch!

"Now this guy grabbed me, which I thought was kina ill-advised; stupid actually. He grabbed me [by the lapel] with the right hand and was talkin' shit; stickin' that jaw out. His left hand was down, not where it 'sposed ta be—and The Mac Daddy punch, punch fo' keeps: right, left, right, all heavy in the jaw. He fell out face-first in the pavement with a broke jaw.

"Chump pressed charges. I goin' ta court at eight-thirty ta represent maself. The company lawyer don' work but so many hours 'fore he cost, en I owe 'im fo' the last assault case."

The Mac Daddy's last semipro football game was against a team consisting of cops. He was ejected and banned from the league for fouls, late hits, and excessive contact. He was, of course, innocent of each of these false allegations. Just ask his mother.

THE CAPITOL HEIGHTS BOYZ

**Time of occurrence: day
Duration: under a minute
Perspective: The Mac Daddy, first-person defender**

"This was started by four members of a gang, in school, in Capitol Heights, Maryland. The Mac Daddy was a course innocent of bad intentions. [Of course, he was innocent!] At the time I'm wrestlin' 159; went ta the state finals. So I'm walkin' around at 170, en these dudes all somewhat smaller.

"They was tryin' ta recruit me. Now The Mac Daddy has his [criminal] friends, but he ain't no gang person—'specially no chump school gang. They say that I gotta join or they gonna kick ma ass. So it's on, right there in the hallway on the top floor.

"I was doin' okay with the punches, but I was caught out in the open. Eight hands 'gainst two just ain't happenin'. So I decide to do somethin' drastic to preserve the situation. I look fo' the smallest chump—short dude—grab the back of his head en ran him past me en threw him into the wall. However, unknown to The Mac Daddy is the fact of a window, which this chump go through and land on the pavement [two stories] below.

"That ended that. The school police had us in cuffs. The dude had a broken hip, jaw, concussion, and dislocated shoulder. I coulda been in serious trouble—shoulda seen how bad this dude looked when they wheeled him into court—but this older lady teacher saw the whole thing and testified on my behalf."

ONE SICK BASTARD

Time of occurrence: day
Duration: under a minute
Perspective: Donnie, eyewitness

"This was in the Towson facility. We were in the common room watching TV—about half white, half black—when this guy starts griping about changing the channel. This guy was one sick bastard—he had raped and killed this crippled girl and left her in the woods. We hated that fucker. A little guy really.

"Well, he gets into it with this big black dude over the TV and calls him a nigger! I thought, *Now that's real smart.*

"The black dude picks him up and dunks him head first into this big, rubber trash can. Everybody was sayin', 'Kill the sick bastard' and cheerin'. So he grabs the guy by the ankles and starts pounding his head into the bottom of the trash can like he's using a posthole digger and just left him there [limp] with his legs danglin' out of the trash can."

SNAP, CRACKLE, POP

Time of occurrence: night
Duration: minutes
Perspective: eyewitness

Three smaller drunks wielding beer bottles attacked Grant, a bouncer and former college linebacker, in the parking lot. He threw

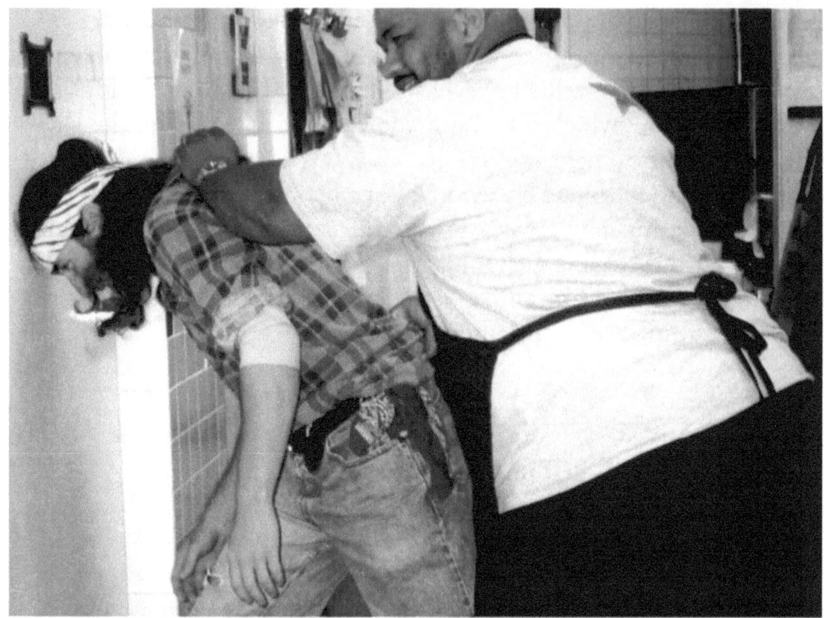

No Neck's door jammer.

No Neck's running bear hug is used to run a smaller man into a building.

Feet's wall scraper.

one man to the asphalt, one over a car, and one through the windshield, incapacitating all three.

This is one of many such incidents I recorded where football players used cartoon-like tactics to incapacitate smaller antagonists.

MOM'S BOYFRIEND

Time of occurrence: day
Duration: seconds
Perspective: first-person aggressor

Quin, a very tall, thin young man, approached a man from behind as he was unlocking the door to his van. Quin grabbed the back of the man's neck, drove his face into the window, and then threw him backward to the pavement with a neck pull and chest push. The man's head bounced off the asphalt, and he lay unconscious in a puddle of blood as Quin headed to the convenience store to get a Pepsi.

Big Earl's windshield smasher. Big Earl weighed in at 410 and tossed a 300-pound man through the windshield of a third party's sports car.

THE MIRACLE OF FLIGHT

**Time of occurrence: day
Duration: seconds
Perspective: Jason, eyewitness**

"The scariest thing I ever saw was these two girls fighting at Owings Mills High School. Both were about the same size, but one girl had the other by the hair with both hands and was whipping her around in circles—completely off the ground—like a parent would swing a kid around by the arms. This was right in the hallway. When she got up a lot of velocity and the other girl was flying parallel with the floor, she let go and launched her into a row of lockers. It was horrible."

"132 POUNDS A TWISTED STEEL EN SEX APPEAL!"

**Time of occurrence: night
Duration: under a minute
Perspective: eyewitness**

I was seated in the lunchroom with the other members of a night crew in a supermarket. White Pimp Chocolate, 5 feet, 8 inches and 132 pounds, and Archie, an aspiring poet, 6 feet, 6 inches and 270 pounds, were arguing about Archie's beloved girlfriend, whom White Pimp Chocolate wanted to add to his already well-stocked harem of ho's. The animosity between these two was long running, and things went physical in a hurry.

The lunchroom was 6 x 10 feet. Archie advanced for a frontal choke, which resulted in a twisting clinch. White Pimp Chocolate countered with a waist tackle and drove the big man up against the wall between the Coke machine and the scheduling board. Archie bent forward for a reverse waist lock, only to be heaved off his feet. As Archie's feet slapped back down on the floor, his eyes bugged out as he said to me, "He picked me up!"

I remarked, "He's taking you down—better call it."

Archie's look of surprise turned to one of horror as he realized that he was about to become the shortest man in the room. Archie tapped, and White Pimp Chocolate strutted to his seat rapping about "slappin' ho's en slayin' giants."

BY MUTUAL AGREEMENT

Time of occurrence: day
Duration: more than a minute
Perspective: Jason, first-person aggressor

"This was at a gas station. I was delivering seafood, and this black guy wouldn't let me out. He was about Mike Tyson's size. [Jason is 5 feet, 8 inches and 170 pounds.] I kept honking the horn, to which he replied, 'Fuck you.'

"I said, 'No, you didn't say that!'

"We both got out. It was snowing, and he was standing uphill from me. I went stupid and kicked him. He grabbed my leg, slammed me to the ground, and started punching me. He definitely knew what he was doing. He rocked me, and I wrapped my legs around his neck. He was picking me up by jerking back and slamming my shoulders on the pavement. He was incredibly strong but started saying, 'It's cool. We can end it.'

"I was like, 'Fuck you!' and was hooking him to the face and ears. Then we heard the sirens and, as if by mutual agreement, got up and pretended we didn't know what was going on."

The jerk slam.

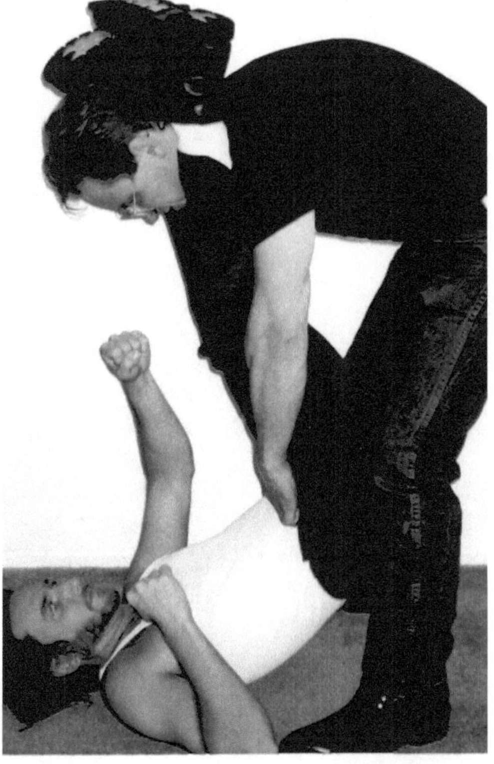

CHAPTER SIX

UPSIDE YO HEAD

A Moment of Moral Silence for the Sucker Punch

> "Human beings are fragile,
> watery things."
> —Larry Niven, *The Magic Goes Away*

Evidence that lower primates punch one another exists in the form of a video in which a chimp punches a baboon in the stomach. Did the chimp think of this on his own, or had he been watching too much TV? Would I uncover any interspecies primate boxing in my study? Lucky for me, I ran into Robert. After my interview, I understood how thrilled a paleontologist might be over an unexpected find.

CINDY IN THE RAFTERS WITH A JOINT

Time of occurrence: day
Duration: seconds
Perspective: Robert, eyewitness/defender

"I was a combat engineer attached to a Special Forces battalion [in Vietnam]. We were up in the Highlands where they had these monkeys. Pretty ornery things. They didn't like the Vietnamese because they knew they wanted to eat them. But some GIs took monkeys as pets.

"This one fella had a monkey named Cindy, who used to drink

beer and smoke pot and lived in his hooch. One day she hid in the rafters and, when the cleaning girl came to clean the hut, Cindy attacked her—bit a chunk out of her hip. I walked up when I heard the scream, and there's Cindy, standin' in front of the hut with a joint in one hand and a beer in the other, snarlin' at me. Now, imagine a thing like that—and then imagine it attacking you! I popped the monkey with a jab, and she backed off.

"The guy was pretty upset when he found Cindy with a black eye. But, man, you have to defend yourself."

DEELO'S PAW

Time of occurrence: night
Duration: seconds
Perspective: Krinkle, eyewitness

"Deelo was one a the New York Boyz. He neva punched. Come up from behine and smack ya with a half-clenched fist. He was sooo strong, slapped a dude durin' a basketball game once en left a bloody hand print on 'is back. His bones was heavy. Looked exactly like Tyson, only uglia, even uglia then Leon Spinx!

"One time we out whit da Dawgz [Deelo's clique] en dis rival dude who Deelo always whooped on was workin' one a da little Dawgz. Deelo come up from behine whit da paw to da right cheek— sent him down! Den out come the .22, en Deelo caps da backa da head, walks ova, en walks on—like that."

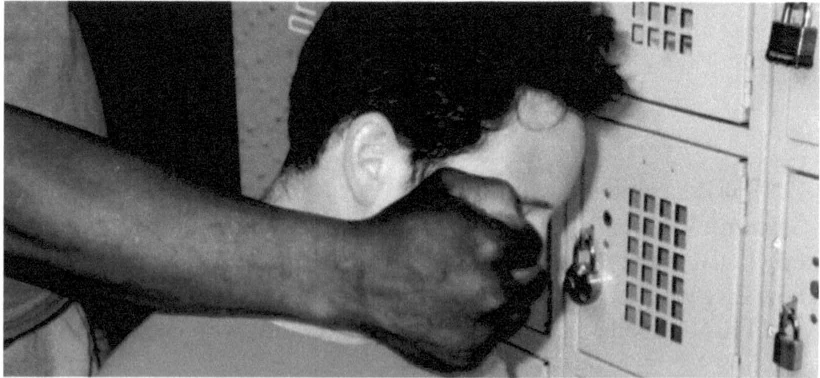

Deelo's paw.

CHAPTER SEVEN

SHINING SHOES

Footwear as a Weapon

"One guy was punching him while
three other guys were stomping all the
loose parts . . . and three to four guys
are stomping his buddy, picking parts—
they knew what they were doing—
ankles, hands, anything that was out."

—Dan

AT THE EDGE OF THE HERD

Time of occurrence: night
Duration: minutes
Perspective: Tattoo Rick, first-person defender

"I was 25 and had stopped drinking because of my stomach problems. This was back when the city had the gun buy-back thing going. I was working down at the GM plant. It was after last call at the bar, a cool fall night. I was with these two guys, on a little street in Fells Point, at the time when there were a lot of vacant houses there. We were headed back to our bikes, which we had parked up from the market. They were walking down the street, and I was slightly behind and to their right on the narrow sidewalk.

"I sensed somebody behind me and felt something poke me in the back. I instinctively came around with the right elbow and caught him in the temple. He dropped, and I heard the clatter of a gun. I said, 'You mutherfucker! I'm gonna fuckin' kill you!'

"This was back when I was wearing the big biker/engineer boots,

The robber's kick.

so I'm stomping the shit out of this guy. That's when my buds came up and said, 'What are ya doin'?'

"I said, 'This guy tried ta rob me so I'm killin' him.'

"They're like, 'Cool dude,' and started stompin' him until they got bored and then kept going. When the person being stomped stops making noise, it kinda takes the fun out of it. The 'Oh, please' phase only lasts 10 to 15 seconds. After that it's just an exercise in futility—just stretching your legs. That's why I always liked those steel-toe boots. A round kick with one of those in your ribs really changes your world.

"I wasn't finished with him—he was still breathing. I played soccer with his head until my legs cramped. The other guys came back, and they're like, 'Come on, man, we aren't standing here all night while you stomp this guy.'

"I put a couple of stomps on his head, took the gun, stuck it in my belt, and joined them. When you walk in places like that and aren't prepared, ugly things happen to you. When you are prepared, fun things—like this—happen. When we got home, my buds said, 'Hey, man, let's see the gun.'

"So I pulled it out and checked the clip. It was empty. Then I slid the action back to check the chamber, and these fuckin' springs popped out—like boiiing! And I said, 'Look at this. This fuckin' idiot tried to rob me with a broken gun with no bullets in it! He deserves what he got.'

"The next day I got the gun back together and took it down to the police station. I felt really cool, riding a motorcycle and packing heat! I was hoping the cops would pull me over. I had the gun stuck in my belt in plain view. I walked into the station with this thing hanging out of my belt and said, 'Do you guys want this?'

"They were like, 'Yeah,' and asked me where I got it.

"'I beat the shit out of some guy in Fells Point and took it from him.'

"'Yeah, right. So what are you, some kind of karate guy?'

"'Yeah, as a matter of fact, I am.'

"So I told them the whole story, and they gave me the $50. I was hoping the thing wouldn't fall apart in their hands. It was a big .45 auto.

"I must not have killed the guy, because the police took all the information. I was kind of surprised about that. He was just some skinny white guy, and I left him with his hair matted to his face with blood. Years later two detectives came to my house asking where I got the gun. They said, 'Yeah, that's what it says here,' and left.

"You never forget a good stomping. I love that sound: that 'melon hitting the concrete' sound. When you hear it, it's like, *Ooh yeah, I got a good one!* It's just like when you hit a golf ball just right.

"I don't feel bad about it. I'm a Darwinist. Why is this guy even on my planet? He's breathing my air, taking up my space. Let's thin the herd. Drive the ones like this to the edge so the predators can eat them. Maybe I fucked this guy up so bad that he couldn't pay his drug debt, and his dealer whacked him. Here comes another one that's getting close to the edge of the herd [points to elderly, enfeebled, alcoholic patron entering the bar with a walker]. 'Good evening, sir. What will it be tonight? A fine mass-produced American brew perhaps?'"

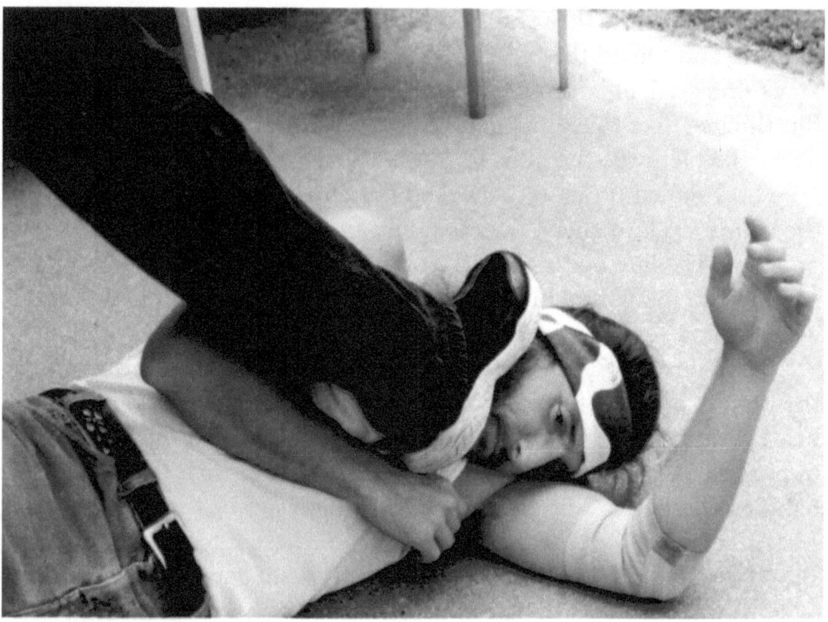

The lunge stomp.

The curb stomp.

The toe stomp is used for raking and slashing the face.

The crunch stomp.

The jump stomp.

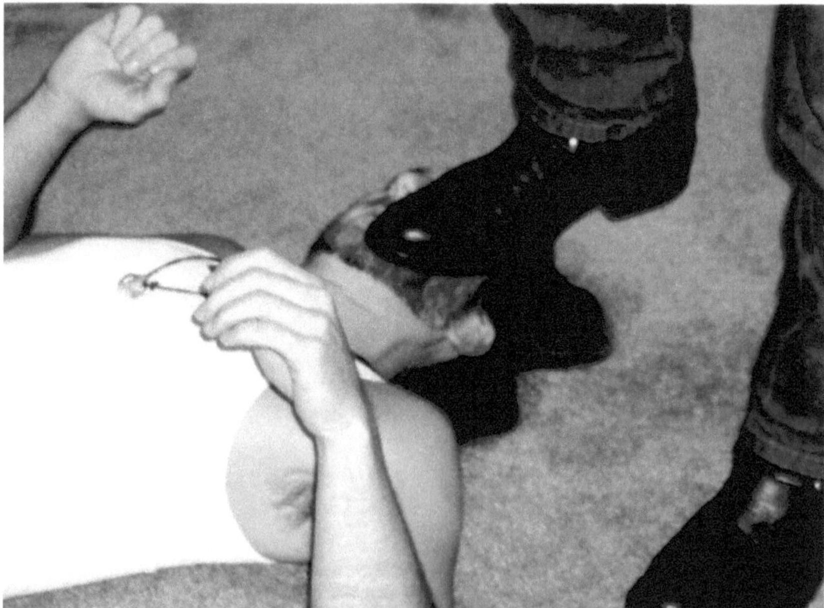

The side stomp is used for slashing with the outside edge of a hard sole.

The kick starter uses the kicker's butt muscles and hamstrings to apply more force.

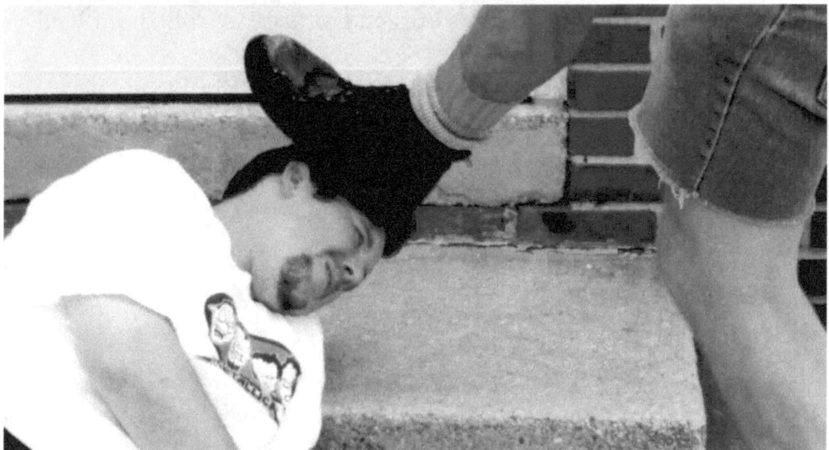

The heel stomp.

WELCOME TO THE JUNGLE, ROMEO

Time of occurrence: night
Duration: minutes
Perspective: The Mac Daddy, first-person aggressor

"When it comes to bidness time, I got these two dudes—real vicious dudes, can't even let them eat at the table. When we go to work, it's we bump and you grind.

"Now The Mac Daddy used to be associated with Big Daddy Dee, much larger en more viciouser than The Mac Daddy. One day Big Daddy go by the McDonalds and see this pretty boy with 'is wife, en make the call. The message a the jungle go out [hollow logs have been replaced by cell phones], en the law a the jungle about to be enforced [no notable technological advancements here]. We locked the doors at about 9:00 P.M. en told the manager not ta worry, no harm to none not involved.

"There was five dudes there. First come the punches, then the smackdown [throw], then Cole whip out the asp [telescopic baton], en said, 'Hold 'im up!'

"Two dudes held him up, en he cracked him across the face. Then came the stompin'. The boy paid triple for his offense—might even get him into heaven. It was a slap stompin'—stompin' him like he was a cockroach. The stompin' went on long enough fo' The Mac Daddy to finish the pretty boy's burger. Even so, we rolled out well ahead of the cops.

"Now the cops, they try ta lay it on Dee. But Big Daddy was laid up wit dis girl the whole time, en she was there in court ta say so. The law of the jungle, brutha—it collects all debts and pays no dues. Justice plain en simple."

In Baltimore and Washington, D.C., the perennial animosity between law enforcement and the black community has fostered a code of silence that encourages vigilante justice.

CHAPTER EIGHT

HITTING THAT MESSY HOME RUN

Clubs

> "Noah is stronger than the bear. For he
> has a club ..."
>
> —J.-H. Rosny Sr., *Quest for Fire*

For this study I defined the club as a weighted stick and broke clubs into four subclassifications:

1. Bats of all kinds
2. Crude (e.g., boards, tree limbs, guitars)
3. Metal (any metal club not defined as a tool;
   primarily bars, pipes, golf clubs)
4. Handy (e.g., brass knuckles, saps, whip sticks, blackjacks)

The club, or weighted stick, has some distinguishing contextual characteristics:

- It is most likely to incapacitate.
- It is most likely to be wielded by members of an attacking group.
- Its use generally does not result in criminal penalties.

THE DILEMMA OF THE CLUB

Based on many of the incidents that I documented, most of which did not make it into this book, many of the clubbers actually injured people more seriously than they had intended. Irene's brother and Joey, described below, are examples of this.

It seems that the high level of energy used to employ these weapons deadens the wielder's appreciation of the damage he has inflicted. The length of bats, at least, did seem to make disarms more attainable by the defender than against smaller weapons, although this is often complicated by the presence of accomplices assisting the batter or wielding bats of their own. The best thing to remember is that the clubber, more often than the users of most other types of weapons, is acting as a member of a violently aggressive group.

DUKE'S REVENGE

**Time of occurrence: night
Duration: under a minute
Perspective: first-person aggressor**

"I wanted that punk-muthufuca bad . . . real bad. My partner found out where he live. No cause for the law—this was personal. We took a drive one night. He live in a nice enough area—nice houses, driveways. His car in the driveway, en we pull up behine as 'is punk-ass is comin' down the driveway.

"Caught the punk-bitch right by the side of 'is car en got the bat on 'im. I had brought the bat. No betta weapon for settlin' scores. I worked 'is punk-ass good: cryin', crawlin', beggin' like a bitch all the way up the driveway. Busted 'im in the legs, arms, elbows, kneecaps—any joint. I wen' fo' a head shot, en ma partner pull me off, told me I didn' wanna do that.

"Left 'is punk-ass lay. Wouldn't be bustin' folks with beer glasses no more."

THE WIFE BEATER

Time of occurrence: night
Duration: seconds
Perspective: eyewitness

Alex heard a drunken neighbor beating his wife in the street at 2:00 A.M. He walked outside and said, "Don't hit a woman; hit a man." The wife beater picked up a 2 x 4 out of the gutter and hit Alex in the thigh and then in the side of the head. The side stroke to the head tore off half his ear and sent him face first to the pavement, where he lay dead with a broken jaw. The paramedics arrived in time to revive Alex. He remained in a coma for two weeks and is permanently disabled. His assailant did 2 1/2 years in jail for the attack and, as soon as he was released, broke an old man's arm in a fight.

BIG MAMA

Time of occurrence: day
Duration: under a minute
Perspective: eyewitness

Ellen was beating up another young lady in the girl's front yard when the victim's mother emerged from the house with a 2 x 4. Ellen and the spectators fled.

HAYNES

Time of occurrence: day
Duration: under a minute
Perspective: first-person defender

"When I was a young man, this guy thought he would rob me on the street 'cause he was bigga than me. I ran down the alley and grabbed a 2 x4 . Brought it down right ova 'is head—down the middle. Stitches, concussion. Wore a space helmet ta court, en the judge made me apologize for it—like I was wrong for not lettin' him rob me."

LITTLE JOEY

Time of occurrence: day
Duration: second
Perspective: Joey, first-person aggressor

At age 14, Joey was getting sick of being bullied by the likes of Darby, a 21-year-old who had just shaken him down for his pocket change and was not beyond putting out his cigarette on the boy's chest. As Joey tells it:

"I picked up this 2 x 4 and hid behind a shed in the alley. When Darby walked by, I took a full swing—I played baseball—and hit him square between the shoulder blades. There was a good, solid thud, and he just fell forward and lay there like he was dead. I panicked and ran. I don't think he ever knew who did it."

HITTING THAT MESSY HOME RUN

Time of occurrence: night
Duration: minutes
Perspective: Donnie, first-person aggressor

"We were out drinking on a corner on Route 40, in Edgewood. The guy I was with was huge, real tall. We were about 20. On our way out, we got into an argument with these five younger guys—16, 17—and got out and fought them. We were havin' a good ol' time. I'm punchin' the shit outta this guy, and my buddy's killin' the others: one under his arm, one by the hair—pounding his face into the car.

"We had won, and this guy came runnin' back with a bat, goin' after my buddy. He was afraid, swingin' that thing like he was a wild man. My buddy was tryin' to fend him off with his hands out in front of him, and the guy hit him across the palm and broke his hand. I came runnin' up behind, and he must have seen me comin', because he turned and swung at me while I was flyin' through the air and hit me right here [point of skull above the forehead].

"I blacked out for an instant when I hit the ground. When I got up, all I saw was blood streamin' down in front of my face. I wasn't good for anything after that, and I could see him comin' at me through the blood, so I just got up and ran. We ran to a friend's house, where somebody called an ambulance, which took me to Falston Hospital. I had a splittin' headache until I got to the hospital; then the real pain started.

"I wasn't workin' at the time and didn't have any insurance. They didn't give me any pain medication, not even Tylenol for the headache. They took this thing that looked like a dent popper—you know, the things they use to fix dented cars—with a wood screw on the end of it, screwed it into my head, and pulled. All I could hear was bone crackin', and the pain was shootin' through my head. *There had actually been a dent in my head.* They put 37 big, wide stitches in my head and kicked me out the next day.

"I didn't have a regular doctor. No money. No insurance. I had a terrible headache for a while. I ended up taking out the stitches myself."

IRENE

Time of occurrence: day
Duration: seconds
Perspective: eyewitness

"I was going over my sister's friend's house in East Baltimore when I ran into my brother, who said he wanted to go with me so he could make a phone call. He knew my sister's friend, so I didn't think nothin' of it.

"When we got inside, they started to argue over some drug-related dispute, and instead of making a phone call my brother goes downstairs. My sister's friend stooped down to work on a television cable, and my brother came back up from the basement with a bat, stepped behind him, and hit him in the right side of the head. The guy went down, and I intervened, pushing my brother back. He was so strong—crazed on some kind of drug—that it was hard to push him back.

"My brother picked up an ashtray and hit the guy on the same spot, and it swelled up. He then turned and said, 'You take that jewelry off [of him], or I'm gonna finish him off!'

"I took off the man's jewelry, gave it to my brother, and made the ambulance call. The ambulance got the victim to the hospital, where he later died.

In the kill zone: the proper stance for achieving nirvana against a clubber.

"I talked to the homicide detective. He said that he knew I was innocent, that it wasn't my fault, and that it was a hell of a thing for my brother to put me in that position. I testified against him, and he got 20 years.

"I had to eventually move away from my family, so I can't go in my old neighborhood anymore. My parents are with the Lord. Half of my family and my brother's friends are against me because I testified. The other half of my family and my sister's friends are against me because I took my brother to the house. But how was I to know his intentions? My brother even had his girlfriend with him at the time—and don't you know, it didn't bother her!"

POOR MISTER HALL

**Time of occurrence: night
Duration: minutes
Perspective: Gus, eyewitness**

"This was at a supermarket and involved an assistant manager, Mister Hall, who liked to mess with people. He messed with me, but I didn't mind. I'm easygoin'. He mess with this young boy, 17, hang with 'em nappy-heads [Jamaicans]. He would write the boy up for small stuff en give him the dirty jobs.

"I knew the boy was angry and tried to calm him down. The boy said, 'I know I need the job, but I can't take this anymore.'

"The next night Mister Hall left at 10:30. I could see him walkin' to his car on the lot—I was inside, night crew. Every time he moved, these two black cars with lights moved.

"Just as he was nearin' his car, they pulled on eitha side, and four dudes with bats got outta each car. They all had bats! Mister Hall was a big man. These dudes were younger, somewhat smaller Jamaicans dressed in black ski masks.

"Oh my God! Poor Mister Hall! They batted him down. Batted him down bad! They was comin' down straight [bent over the fallen man], and you could hear the hit from inside. It was terrible. No man deserves to be done like that unless he harm a chyle.

"I had called the police—didn't even think about goin' out there. Not only for the bats—if you got eight Jamaicans, you got at least two guns! I thought they had killed Mr. Hall. There was no sign of life when they stopped.

"Mister Hall lived. He was in the hospital for six weeks: broke arms, broke ribs, jaw broke in four places, plate in 'is head. The police did investigate, but the boy's mother swore he was home with her the whole time. No charges against no one."

DEELO'S CREW

(Summary of various eyewitness and first-person accounts.)

"The Dawgz was a vicious crew. They three bruthas from New York: ruthless, big, tall, thick dudes. DeeLo was the one ta watch fo'. He'd hit ya first from the sneak, en then things happened. They could fight, en they oways used a whipstick: a fishing weight attached to a clothes hanger en wound up with black plastic tape.

"There was DeeLo with the sneaky paw, Eli pack the .22, en Tone—he had a black snake he fed white rats to. They'd fight ya first. The .22 was for when things got outta hand. DeeLo cap five dudes I knew of; one died. I knew 'im to knock out three dudes by whip-stickin'. They was a bad crew. They outta state now, en I heard that DeeLo is dead. He didn't make many friends."

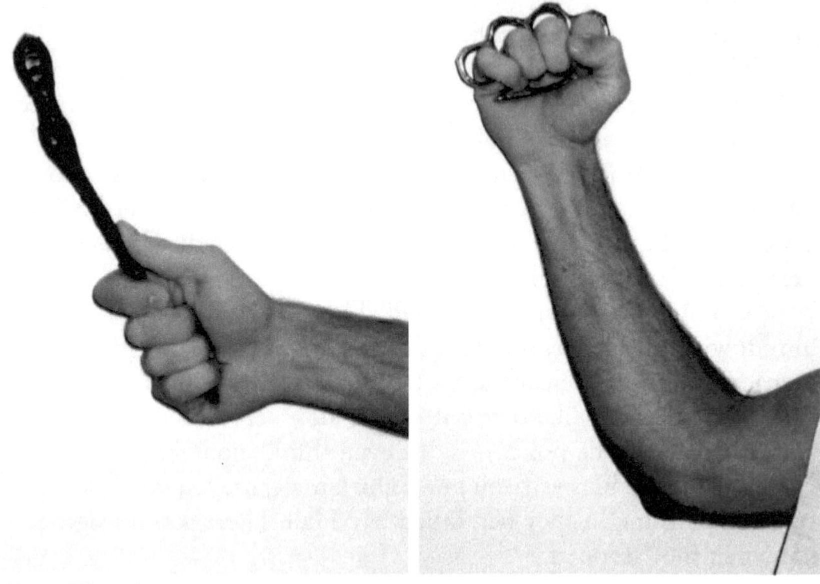

Above: The whipstick.

Above right: Brass knuckles—classified along with saps, blackjacks, and whip-sticks—are handy purpose-made bludgeons.

THE FOURTH REICH

Time of occurrence: night
Duration: under a minute
Perspective: Link, first-person aggressor

"My friend Steve, we were in the Fourth Reich together, had been jumped by these mookes [blacks], and they broke a bat over his head. We went out one night, six of us with two bats, and caught these seven mookes out in the open. I've never been in a fight during the day—ever. It's mostly at night and outside. The bat is such a fun weapon. We had three of these guys hurt, and two were down while the rest scattered like rats in fire. The sound of a bat hitting ribs is very distinctive, sounds just like popcorn popping. What a perfect night that was."

LAZARUS

**Time of occurrence: day
Duration: minutes
Perspective: first-person defender**

Lazarus was walking past a rundown rental property when he was attacked by a pit bull that wrestled him to the ground. As the dog literally ate his left hand, the big man methodically broke the dog's legs with his right hand. He managed to drag himself and the dog within reach of a 2 x 4, which he used to beat the dog to death. He lost the two small fingers of the left hand.

DENNY

**Time of occurrence: night
Duration: minute
Perspective: first-person defender**

Denny owed money to his dealer, who, along with two men armed with bats, cornered him in an East Baltimore alley and beat him. At the time of the interview, Denny was confined to a wheelchair due to skeletal and neurological damage and was attempting to regain the use of his body through physical therapy.

TANGO

**Time of occurrence: night
Duration: seconds
Perspective: first-person defender**

Tango was drinking in a bar with a friend who got into an argument with one of the locals. On the way out, Tango was attacked by a small man with a bat. He blocked the downstroke with his left forearm, grabbed the bat with that hand between the batter's hands, grabbed the head of the bat with his right hand, and wrenched the weapon free, discarding it as they left. His left forearm was injured but not broken.

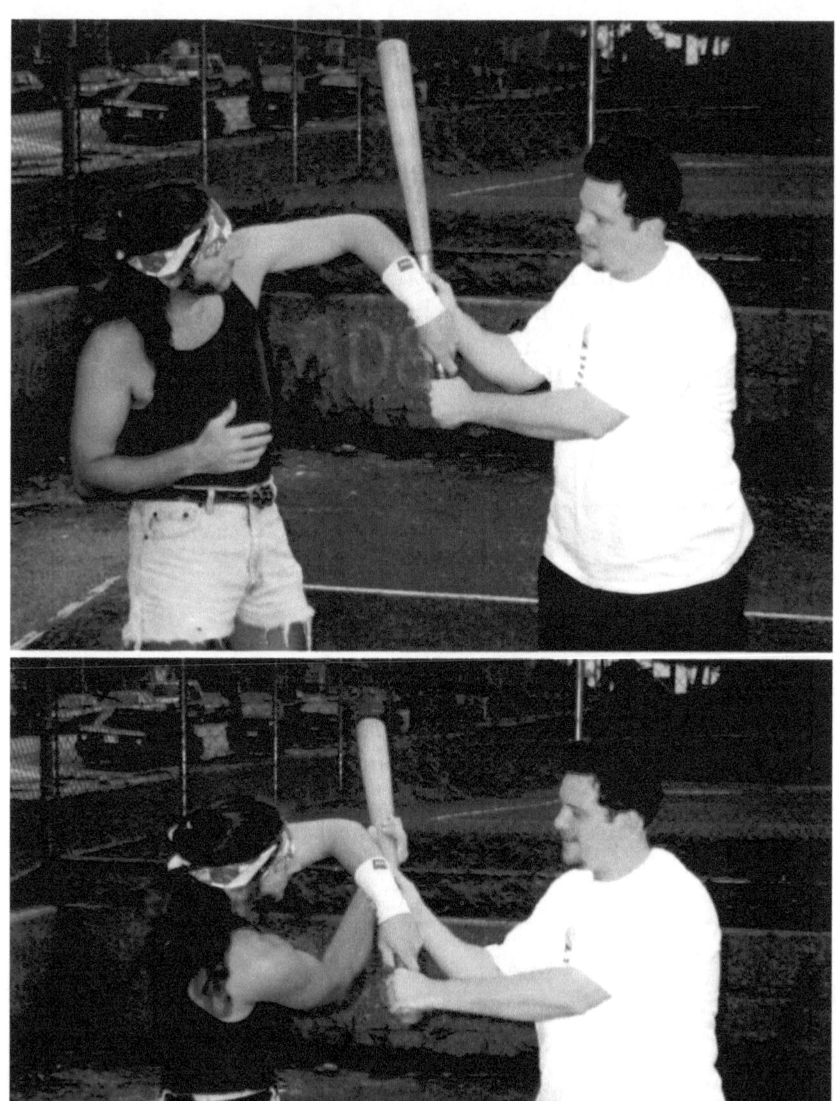

Tango's bat grab.

OUTSIDE THE HARBOR INN

**Time of occurrence: night
Duration: minutes
Perspective: first-person aggressor**

Tango had agreed to back "the stupid brother of this cute girl I was seeing" in a fight outside a notorious dive. Both parties grabbed what was at hand, leaving Tango with a rubber hose with a hard knob on the end. After the primary enemy—a large, muscular man with a steel bar—disabled the brother and Tango's cute girl was neutralized by an enemy female, he was left to face the big man with the steel bar.

Trying to talk his way out of the fight, Tango agreed to drop the hose, only to have the big man go for his head with a diagonal downstroke. Tango employed his bat grab, suffering a fracture of the radial bone, and found himself unable to twist the bar free from the big man's hands. They grappled and talked until Tango convinced the big man that he had just been there to make sure the girl's brother had not been ganged up on. They agreed to a truce, and Tango collected his wounded and cleared out.

WALKING TALL

Sticks and Violence

Generally speaking, the stick offers less legal risk to the user than any other weapon, as long as it has not been altered into a club by additions to the striking end. Like clubs, sticks are often used by members of aggressive groups. As a weapon, many sticks lack lethal potential in the hands of the untrained but, like clubs, sometimes lend themselves to overkill tactics in the hands of excited wielders.

A burned rattan fighting stick and a hardwood baton, both classified as sticks for this study.

KENNETH

Time of occurrence: night
Duration: more than a minute
Perspective: first-person aggressor

"It was in Northeast Baltimore, workin' security; sure enough in the 'hood. I walked up on 'im stealin'. Young hopper walkin' with a big stick—'bout 4 feet long, could barely get your hand around it. He's a tall, junkie-lookin' guy, 33 or so, tearin' open a pack of Nicorettes.

"I walked up on 'im like, 'Man, what the hell you think ya doin? Inquirin' mind wanna know what the hell you doin'?'

"He says, 'Fuck you, man!'

"Then he try ta run. I grab the stick. We was battlin' for the stick up against the wall by the fire extinguisher. It was the closest thing I was to. I had him against the wall with my right hand, grabbed the fire extinguisher with me left—pulled the pin with one hand—and let him have it! He went down like a chicken with its head cut off, sayin', 'I can't breathe!'

"I said, 'Damn right, you can't breathe. Put yo hands behind ya before I bust yo ass!'

"When I on duty, I got the law on my side . . . long as I don't go too far."

RAPHAEL

Time of occurrence: night
Duration: minutes
Perspective: Raphael, first-person aggressor

When Raphael and four other bouncers ejected six muscleheads, one had promised Raphael that they would come back for him. They kept their word. Raphael explains how he used a car antenna and his arnis skills to defend himself against their attack later that night.

"The club officially closes at 2:00 A.M. As I came out at about 3:00 A.M., I didn't see them. They were parked 'round the side. As I headed to my car, the one who had threatened me came around to my left, running his mouth, 'This en this en this—I'm gonna kick your butt.' And so on.

"One guy was standing back by the car with a bat. The one I had shin-stomped was right in front of me because he thought he was so much bigger than me. I could see there was no way I was going to get to my car. I said, 'What you gonna do with that bat?'

"'Put it upside yo head!'

"I said, 'No, you ain't. You got a real conflict of interest.'

"He says, 'I'll conflict your interest, you taco-vending wetback!'

"The batman came around to my left, and the rest of their boys backed them up in a semicircle. The bouncers came out to back me up, all four of them. I said to the guy, 'Why don't you leave?'

"'Fuck you!' he said.

"'Is this your car?' I asked as I snapped off the antenna. This was the first time I ever used an antenna in a fight. I already had one on me. Now I could go double-stick. Master Billy Bryant taught me this. I said, 'You wanna go? You want a war? You feel like Freddy the Frog, then jump.'

"People get real brave when they're on that juice [steroids]. I went into the sinawali and whipped him up real good while his boys watched—whacked him six or seven times, and he started to run.

"Feet then went up to the batman and asked, 'What are you gonna do with that?'

"That's when they all ran. They were pathetic. Of all the street fights I've been in, I've hardly ever been tested on a martial level. When you fight a man in the ring, you are tested. After that, fighting some juiced-up whiteboy on the street is just like taking out the trash—just cleaning up a mess."

DAVE THE COP

Time of occurrence: day
Duration: seconds
Perspective: first-person aggressor

"I was walking a foot beat in West Baltimore—this was awhile back—and this crowd of darkies were loitering. When I told them to disperse, they were mostly cooperative, except for this one really big sum-bitch who decided to give me some shit. I brought that stick down over his head and opened him up like a watermelon. That was that—didn't give me any shit after that."

GINA THE CRUEL

Time of occurrence: day
Duration: seconds
Perspective: eyewitness

During a teenage game of show-and-tell in a neighborhood basement, Ed exposed himself and approached Gina, arms outspread, saying, 'I love you.' Gina grabbed a yellow wiffle ball bat and struck the erect organ with an audible smack. Ed lay incapacitated for many long, lonely minutes as his friends howled with laughter.

MUGGING BIG DON

Time of occurrence: night
Duration: seconds
Perspective: eyewitness

Little Shoe, a small, unpopular drunk, decided to wait outside the Black Glove bar to exact some revenge on Big Don, his latest tormentor. Emerging from the bar, Big Don caught the umbrella that Little Shoe had swung overhand in both hands, muscled Shoe around, and slammed him into the brick wall, knocking him out.

BRADLEY

Time of occurrence: night
Duration: seconds
Perspective: Bradley, first-person defender

"I was 24, drinking in Mother's Strip Club in Fort Worth, Texas. About 1:30 in the morning, I went up to this guy playing pool and asked him where the bathroom was. He put the tip of the cue in the corner pocket and snapped off the heavy end of the stick. I remember thinking to myself, *That's stupid,* and then he hit me in the side of the head. I was out. My buddy had left. A girl got me outside, telling me that they were going to throw me in a ditch out in the country. I had thrown up and gone into convulsions. She took me home.

"When I woke up, my hair was matted with blood and my pillow soaked all the way through—squish. I felt the side of my head, and it was soft, mushy like a sponge. My wife said, 'We can't afford to take you to the hospital.' But I knew I had to go, so I called my mom.

"The doctor said, 'We're goin' to get an X-ray.' I had the most excruciating headache of my life, and this guy comes running out of the X-ray room, exclaiming, 'Oh my God, did you see the guy with the head injury?' He had hit me so hard that the skull had fractured in seven places just above the ear. If he had hit me lower, the eye would have popped out. It had cracked so good, it had drained itself. The doctor said it was pure luck that I was alive, and that being drunk had helped by thinning the blood.

"They put me on a gurney and put me in next to this Mexican dude whose friend had caught him humping his wife and shot him in the ass with a short .22, and they were trying to extract it. I could see my mom and dad crying. The doctor said that I was the luckiest person he had ever seen. If I hadn't been busted so good, I would have died in my sleep. I spent three or four days in the hospital.

"I never really saw the guy's face—could tell you he was short and one of three brothers who were known for being bad news. I looked into things a bit after I recovered. All I remember was a flash of light after he snapped off the tip. It was probably best I never went back. I had the name, knew where they lived, but I figured their life would catch up to them some day."

Bradley recovered and is now middle-aged and working as a long-haul trucker.

CHAPTER TEN

ACTING SMALL

Rocks and Rocklike Weapons

> "I rolled on my side and pushed with my feet and shoulders [he had been tied up before being stoned], trying to use my feet and shoulder like a hand to pull away, trying to get under the bushes for protection. I didn't get in them but got close enough to get some protection from the canopy. The rocks fell very close to my head."
>
> —George, a stoning victim

Stoners exhibit much of the same detached behavior as shooters. The target has usually been thoroughly dehumanized. This is about as basic as it gets. Stones provide physical distance, as do guns, thus enabling the aggressor to maintain his distance and discouraging sympathy. God forbid, sympathy for the victim. Stoning was a Biblical method of public execution for a reason.

LORD OF THE FLEAS

Time of occurrence: day
Duration: seconds
Perspective: Tattoo Rick, first-person aggressor

"I would have been 11 or 12. We were Belair Road [U.S. Route 1] boys, four or five of us little guys—punks in training, you might say—hanging out in the woods. In the summer, we used to hide out in the drainage tunnels along the creek that fed into Back River, until the bums starting coming up in them to sleep. They were old-time bums, hobo-style guys with the old clothing. There was really no army surplus attire in those days [early 1960s].

"We were hanging in the woods, and these older boys came by with sticks and a gas can. We asked, 'What are you doing?'

"They were like, 'We're goin' to burn a bum.'

"We were like, 'Can we come?'

"They said, 'Yeah, get some stones.'

"So off we went, as happy as boys can be. We collected our rocks. I always preferred the composite rocks with the little pebbles and gravel sticking out of them to give them a cutting edge. They were disallowed in stone battles—igneous and metamorphic rock only.

"Our job was to stand on top of the tunnel and throw rocks when the bum came out. We were the auxiliary punks. We didn't participate in the actual immolation. They went in when we had our stones piled. They doused him while he was sleeping, lit him up, and came out yelling, 'Get out of here, you bum!'

"The bum was bellowing and yelling threats, chasing them. When he came out on the concrete ledge, he was pretty well engulfed in flames. We commenced pelting him with stones, and he jumped into the collection pool—a pond, really, which was about 50 feet across. Most of the stones were thrown at him while he was swimming to the far side. The concrete ledge to the tunnel was sheer and slick right where the water was deepest.

"The older boys were scattering through the woods. Once I ran out of stones, I ran to my grandmother's house. I was lucky she lived right up the road—the bum was a little upset. We never saw him again."

"I-AM-A-BLACK-BELT!"

Time of occurrence: night
Duration: seconds
Perspective: eyewitness

Steve and Bob were minding their own business in the poolroom of a local bar. As they prepared to leave, a drunken patron approached and challenged Bob to a fight. Bob, who had built a reputation as a young man for winning fights but now avoided violence, declined and turned to leave. The drunk followed and warned Bob that he was a black belt in judo. Bob snatched the cue ball off the table as the drunken judoka advanced, palmed it, and executed a palm strike, hitting the drunk between the eyes with an audible crack. The black belt was knocked out cold.

DONALD

Time of occurrence: day
Duration: seconds
Perspective: first-person defender

"This was uptown, over toward the west side, back when I had the jewelry business. I'm riding the moped through this black area when these six homeboys attacked from all sides—like I'm a fuckin' extra slated for death in a Tarzan movie! I got smacked with a bottle, but it was the brick that really jarred me. Thank god I was wearing a helmet. They even threw one of those metal trash bins at me. I almost wrecked but managed to keep going even though I was injured—and the whole time there's a fucking cop sitting behind me in his cruiser doing nothing.

"I'm injured, and this slacker won't even file a report. I took it all the way to the mayor's office—you know, the genius that wanted to legalize crack and heroin—and all they did was harass me. Well, it turns out I stepped on toes all the way up, because violent crime, especially interracial stuff, is not supposed to get on the books when you're trying to attract tourists to this beautiful city of ours."

POTTS

Time of occurrence: night
Duration: minutes
Perspective: eyewitness

"This was at a group home in Annapolis. A lot of people used to hang out there and get high. There was this one crazy Marine—the kind of guy who breaks up a party with a shotgun—who was out of control.

"Him and these two lesser jerks kicked this old drunk out of the yard. When the guy passed out, they got a brush and can and painted him. Then they started beating him and threw him down into a ravine, where they dropped cinder blocks on him. When they went down there to drag him out, they found him dead. The Marine panicked and said, 'You guys can't say shit. You were all involved.' Nobody wanted to cross him.

"They got a hacksaw, cut off his legs, and buried him. The two accomplices were pretty reluctant—you could say forced—but they were pretty much into the initial beating. The bum had a daughter who looked for him, and a dog eventually dug up a femur bone and took it home. All three of the guys did time. But I bumped into one of the accomplices six months later, and he was pretty much done with it. His brother was a high-powered lawyer. That's pretty light for such a heinous act. I guess it all comes down to who you know in this corrupt world."

BRUTHAS 'N SISTAS

Time of occurrence: night
Duration: various
Perspective: first-person

Jordy was beating a man in the street when he was attacked by two of the victims' female relatives. While the two women pinned Jordy to the asphalt, the man picked up a brick in two hands and smashed him in the chin, breaking his jaw.

About two weeks later—jaw still wired shut—Jordy was feeling pretty sore about having to eat with a turkey baster, when he saw the other man on the street. Jordy chased him down, but the man then produced a bat and clubbed him across the jaw. Jordy was hospitalized and his jaw rewired.

Later that week Jordy and his brothers ambushed the man and bricked him in the face, breaking his jaw. All parties declined to co-operate with the police so that they would be free to pursue their vendettas. A truce was eventually called.

DRINKING AND DRIVING

Time of occurrence: night
Duration: minutes
Perspective: Raphael, first person

"This was on Highway 55 outside of Chicago. We weren't all [Latin] Kings. There were five of us: Tocco, the Mexican boxer; me; Tone; and two other Kings. We were cruising along, and these four white boys sped by and threw a can of beer at us. Tone had to swerve, could have killed us. So we chased these guys for 20 miles. They obviously forgot about us or thought they lost us, because they pulled into this parking lot behind this apartment building and kept drinking.

"We pulled up on the street above them and came down the hill. We had a tire iron, crowbar, bricks, and a cinder block. We attacked from all sides. The block shattered the windshield. Tocco went through the driver's side window with the crowbar and used it to drag the guy out. I shattered the passenger's side window into the guy's face, opened the door, and pulled him out of the car. The others used bricks to break the windows. We stomped the two we dragged out. The other two screamed—it was terrible—and cowered. The passenger had thrown the beer can at us. We let him and the driver lie and took the keys and ditched them."

UTILIZE THAT PREHENSILE THUMB

Improvised Weapons

"Man became man, in part, because he held a weapon in his hand."
—Robert L. O'Connell, *Of Arms and Men*

Let's hear it for mankind! I met the Mac Daddy in 1998, on the night crew of a Baltimore City supermarket. He stood 5 feet, 11 inches and weighed about 340 pounds. He grew up in a tough area of Washington, D.C., and liked to intimidate "Baldamore bruthas" with his ominous street cred. He was the undisputed king of our domain and I his diabolical counselor . . . until Big Shiv came to work as our security guard. Big Shiv was from Turner Station, a black suburb of East Baltimore that dates to the pre–Civil War era. Big Shiv stood 6 feet, 5 inches, weighed in around 450 pounds, and was a self-declared predatory homosexual. At 5 feet, 8 inches and 153 pounds, I found it quite troubling to be standing at the urinal in the men's room when Big Shiv entered, as he was in the habit of whispering seductive threats into the ear of any man caught in this compromised position.

It was not long before The Mac Daddy and Big Shiv decided to fight for territorial dominance. As the resident expert on all things violent, I was approached to sanction their fight. Neither man wanted to be arrested or fired for slugging it out, so I was dragooned into service as the underground fight facilitator. Since we were working in a heavily policed, upscale white enclave, I strongly suggested they not fight outside and away from the Orwellian gaze of the ubiquitous cameras manned by the loss prevention department.

Fortunately for the recently unpunched man-cards of both of these notorious but aging thugs, I found a solution. Our milk cooler was 20 x 24 feet and had no camera inside. I constructed a 16-foot square cage of pallets of crated gallon milk jugs, which permitted each fighter his own separate entrance from either side of the walk-in.

The men met for battle in the middle of the ring and began fighting, according to no set of rules, on my call. I was only there to say "go" and witness the inevitable bad ending. As I hid behind a support beam, like some early mammal observing T-rex battling triceratops, Big Shiv landed a jab-straight combination to the formidable brow ridge of The Mac Daddy. Big Shiv winced in pain as his hands and wrists buckled on contact with the thick, bony shield that was the forehead of The Mac Daddy.

The Mac Daddy was no technician, but he had good instincts. He left his head open and proceeded to punch the soft hands of Big Shiv with his own mutated paws or, as he referred to them, "chump-hammas." Within two minutes, Big Shiv tapped to fist punches and retired with a bruised knuckle, sprained thumb, and sprained wrist.

Later that morning Big Shiv asked me to walk up to the park with him so I could train him for the rematch. As we entered the park, a yipping, 5-pound, white poodle broke from a bun-haired old lady and came prancing toward us. This pooch was so small it could have lived inside one of Big Shiv's size-17 boots. So I was astonished to find Big Shiv literally climbing up my body, standing on my feet, and getting as much of his body above my shoulders as he could. I thought I would snap in half at any moment. The dog's owner looked up in bewilderment, over my head, on top of which Big Shiv's arms were folded, as he pleaded down to her, "Is it a good dog?! Is it a good dog?!"

Needless to say, I decided not to train Big Shiv, but I did make a habit out of interviewing The Mac Daddy at every opportunity.

THAT THANG

Time of occurrence: night
Duration: minutes
Perspective: The Mac Daddy, first-person aggressor

"Ya mean da scar ova da right eye? Oh yeah, dat a chump-scar . . . Ova a ho, ma brutha, ova a ho. Some ho—fine enough fo' The Mac Daddy, but too fine fo' da chump she was wit'. Ya know, bein' a lady a taste she want The Mac Daddy, wantin' ta give up *That Thang*—en the chump don' comprehend dat he outclassed. So The Mac Daddy gotta smack 'im down, where 'is chump-ass belong!

"In the street, ma brutha, in the street—whoopin' dat chump-ass. The Mac Daddy weren't 'is full 280 at dat young age. But he whoopin' ass, ma brutha, whoopin' that nigga's ass!

"No grabbin' o' holdin', no wrasslin' o' any a dat; jus beatin' the reality into 'is chump-ass!

"The Mac Daddy too much fo' da nigga, an da ho fine wit' it. She already lookin' ta lay it up on da table—The Mac Daddy en That Thang was a destination, a realization of The Mac Daddy popalaridy—and da chump couldn't hang wit' dat. So he crack The Mac Daddy upside da head from behine wit' a bottle. That when the ass-whoopin' begin in earnest—nigga payin' en prayin'!

"Then the po-lice sirens. Now, The Mac Daddy nor da chump there to get arrested. So it come time to haul ass! A course, da ho eventually lay That Thang up on da table for The Mac Daddy, en da chump jus got ta deal wit' it. The Mac Daddy happy wit' That Thang and that . . . was that."

I apologize to you students of the English language, but I was feeling misty over a recent separation and just had to include a story with a fairy-tale ending.

LITTLE RONNY SPADE

Time of occurrence: day
Duration: various
Perspective: Little Ronny, first person

"I grew up in the hood. I was 11. The bully was 16—would always chase and beat me. I was getting sick of it. He chased me down this alley one day after school, grabbed me by the collar, and punched me in the back. He still had a hold of me, so I reached out and grabbed a good handful of North Avenue dirt—sand, glass, pebbles, rat shit—and threw it in his eyes, slugged him in the face, kicked him, and ran my ass off!

"Another day he chased me all the way home, and I slammed the door in his face. My brother—early 20s, just out of the Marines—said, 'Go back out there and fight him, win or lose, or I'll kick your ass!'

"I went back out—no question—but didn't realize my brother was behind me. He whipped that boy every which way. I was just the bait—punch, slam, smash . . .

"I said to the bully, 'I told you one day you'd get yours!'

"My brother said, 'Shut up. I ought to whoop your ass too,' and kept workin' this kid over. I enjoyed it. It was a terrible beating, and he was a bully no more."

• • •

The next incident, I suppose, should be considered a chemical weapon usage, but I classified it as a common article encounter. This category includes such things as dirt and hairbrushes but is dominated by cans, bottles, and other containers of liquid. Such things as marble ashtrays and trophies were classified with rocks and bricks, while pencils and pens were classified as shanks.

Manny has worked as a street artist and standup comedian. At the time of this interview, he was operating a tattoo parlor. We conducted this interview at the parlor as he awaited "an oppressed Nubian Prince, who is on his way over here to hurt my 'body." If semantics could kill, I'm sure this guy would be a terror.

An arsenal of improvised weapons in Southwest Baltimore.

Vic the Amazon's hair pick.

MANNY'S JUG

**Time of occurrence: night
Duration: three seconds
Perspective: Manny, first-person aggressor**

"This was the fall of '98 in Curtis Bay. I lived in the end unit of a row. The side of the house, where the kitchen was, faced an alley. People were making drug deals in the alley. You're trying to make a sandwich, and you hear some guy say he's gotta take a piss, and this guy is pissing up against the side of your house. The side of the house smelled like piss. It's not an easy activity to monitor—it's not like they all came and pissed on your house at 9:15 P.M.

"I got a cat litter jug. I was going to use a milk jug, but you could see into it. Besides, the milk jug makes that glug-glug sound—you want a nice, smooth delivery system. The cat litter jug has a wide mouth and holds 2 1/2 gallons!

"I kept this jug in the upstairs bathroom and pissed in it. It's really good to have a jug of piss, in case somebody takes your parking spot. Piss is good. You can do a lot of things with piss.

"It took anywhere from two weeks to a month to fill it. It's not a regular thing. You have to open it to fill it, and that can get pretty nasty. You open a jug of this stuff and it's fermented; it doesn't even smell like piss anymore, really nasty.

"I got home late from work, and I could hear these guys in the alley. This one freak was going to piss on my house. I went to the [kitchen] window, and he was assuming the 'about-to-piss position.' Have you ever noticed that people who are pissing are helpless?

"So I went upstairs to the bathroom, got the jug—which was filled to the rim—opened the lid, swung open the window, and dumped it on this guy from two stories! Not a glug, just a nice even *hiss* as 2 1/2 gallons of steaming-hot, month-old, festering piss washed down his back.

"The guy yelled, 'Ah fuck!'

"I soaked this guy. He ran down the alley yelling that he's going to kill me, but I never saw him again. I had something waiting for him. The wall-pissings stopped, like the passing of an era. That was the end of it—except I spent $40 in long-distance calls telling people about the Great Dumping of the Jug.

"I no longer keep a jug. Some things, though, you want to memorialize, like the black kid with the knife who tried to rob me when I was carrying a gun. After I took his shoes, I kept them in the back of my car for years to show to nonbelievers.

"The only thing that separates tragedy and humor is time and space."

CHAPTER TWELVE

CRUSH! KILL! DESTROY!

Tools, Vehicles, and Furniture as Weapons

> "I don't care how good a fighter you are. If you have a sharp stick and the other guy has a gun, you're pretty much fucked."
>
> —Tattoo Rick

DAN F.

Time of occurrence: night
Duration: under a minute
Perspective: Dan, first-person defender

"It was football season. I was 15, 140 pounds, walking home from my girl's house at about 10:30 P.M, along the side of the road up Benavon Heights [Pittsburg] hill. My older brother had a feud with this group we called the Dirt Bags.

"All of a sudden a maroon LTD four-door pulled up with four of them in it—two to three years older than me, not big for their age, 130 to 160. The passenger side pulls by me, and they slam on the brakes. I picked up my pace as they backed up—kept walking. The passenger asked, 'You Darill's brother?'

"'Yeah,' I replied.

"The driver was getting out, and the passengers were pushing their doors open. The guy in the back seat was hurrying out when I kicked the door into his legs and knocked him back into the car.

When the driver tried to tackle me, I did a standing sprawl and punched him pretty good. Right cross. Good shot. Didn't stop him. The passenger hit me and knocked my glasses off. I hit him with a right cross and the driver with a left hook. I lost my balance trying to deal with two guys at once, and the next thing I know I'm getting kicked and stomped.

"They said, 'Next time it'll be your brother.'

"I was on my knees looking for my glasses—Mom would kill me. A neighbor pulled up and helped me. I went to the hospital: black eye; bloody nose; skinned face, knees, elbows; bruised ribs; tennis shoe mark across my head.

"Darill wouldn't let my mom call the police. He went hunting. A conventional beating on one. His friends beat another. He yanked the driver out through the car window, threw him, and pounded him. I eventually got a one-on-one with the driver."

CINDY AND SPARK

Time of occurrence: night
Duration: seconds
Perspective: first person

"I was waiting for the bus on Eastern Avenue, and this little street person [Spark] with his shopping cart—kind of wiry, red bandana, short-haired old person with a tan—was making comments about my body, wanting to touch me. I was very disgusted. Well, since he didn't get the response he appeared to want, he bumped me with his bag-person cart and knocked me out into traffic in front of the bus. I was almost killed! I walked up the street.

"Later on I told Raphael. The man has given me no more trouble and hasn't tried to kill me with his bag-person cart."

A week later my man Spark, who on various occasions has offered me a swig from his warm 40 at the bus stop, was found jammed headfirst into his cart, with various head and face injuries. Witnesses told me that a Latino man was seen punching and kicking Spark minutes before the police arrived to remove Spark from his trusty conveyance.

THE AVENGING ANGEL OF SOBRIETY

Time of occurrence: day
Duration: minutes
Perspective: Raphael, first-person aggressor

Raphael, with the aid of a cane, had just left outpatient knee surgery at a Chicago hospital. Dressed in his tae kwon do uniform, Raphael was en route to the TKD class he taught. After class, he had to rush to pick up his wife from the airport. Then his evening took a detour . . .

"This sorry-looking, redneck-type of whiteboy cut me off at an intersection. I noticed he was drinking a can of beer. Drunk driving is unacceptable, so I followed him for miles until he pulled into a strip mall and entered a Korean liquor store. I pulled up on the other side of a van. By the time I limped into position, he was exiting the liquor store with a six-pack under his arm and drinking a beer [sneer of disgust].

"He opened the car door, placed his can of beer in the can holder, put the six-pack on the passenger seat, and got in. By the time I got to him, he was seated behind the wheel and pulling the door closed. I used the cane to balance myself as I yanked open the door and reverse-punched him in the face.

"I shoved him back and crawled in on top of him. He was twisted, with his feet under the steering wheel and his head on the six-pack on the passenger seat. I had the mount and was choking him with my left hand while I was palm-striking his chest and hitting him in the face with vertical fists.

"I could hear the sound of his head hitting the six-pack, and I was really upset, screaming at him while I held up my black belt, 'I could kill you! Do you understand? Don't drink and drive!'

"The owners of the store were looking on, so I turned to them and said, in Korean, 'Call the police. I have a drunk driver.'

"They were upset and confused and continued to watch, chattering to each other, mamasan and papasan.

"The drunk was crying and begging, 'Don't kill me. Please don't kill me!'

"I spit in his face and continued to punch him. It was crazy. [You think?] The blood was splashing up my sleeves and onto the dashboard and window. I guess I was a little out of control. You know, you get fed up with these dipsy-do people and all their Mickey Mouse issues. I really don't know how long the entire episode lasted. He started to cry and wiggle—making, 'wee-wee-wee' noises and fluttering his fingers. When he stopped moving, I crawled out of the car, took his can of beer, crawled back inside, and dumped it on his face, 'Drink!' I opened more of his beer and dumped it on him. Then I retrieved my cane and left him there.

"I made it to class on time, my white uniform covered in blood. I taught a good class—*very intense*. The students were very dedicated that day. After class I picked up my wife from the airport. The day was rushed, and I had no change of clothes with me. She was very upset over my appearance."

ED

**Time of occurrence: day
Duration: under a minute
Perspective: eyewitness**

"I was driving Joey home in my beater—he's like a black belt in four different kinds of karate—when these two dudes cut us off and flipped us the bird. We followed a little, and they pulled over and the passenger got out. So did Joey. I didn't exactly see what he did to the guy, but the guy was down and Joey was dragging the body back to my car. I'm like, 'What the fuck?'

"He laid the guy's head on the floorboard next to the seat and slammed the door shut on his face! The head fell out of the car. So he put it back up there and slammed the door shut two more times. We got the fuck out of there. There was blood splashed up on the door and dashboard. I'm thinkin', *Who does that?*"

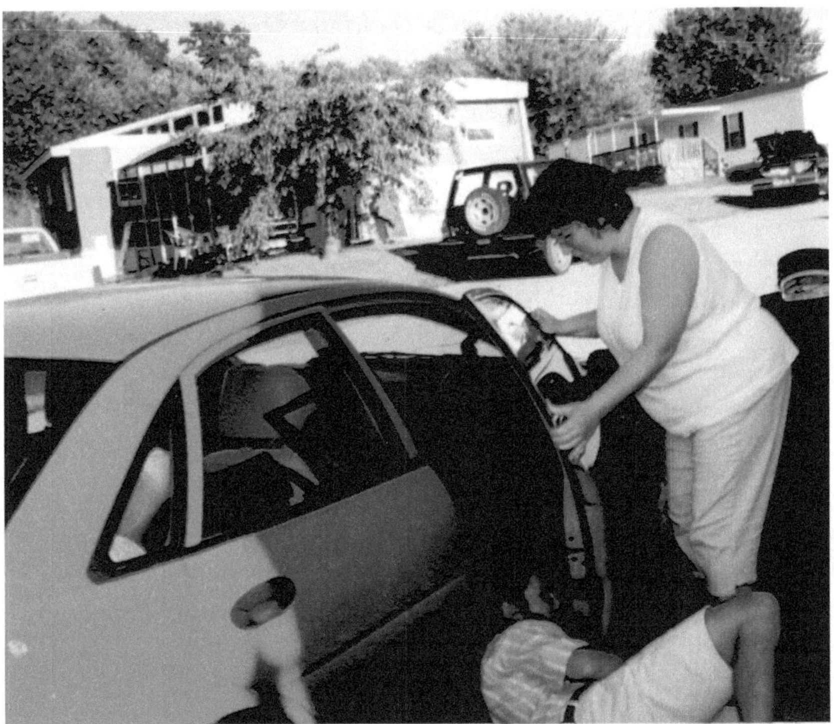

Finishing with the car door.

LINK

Time of occurrence: night
Duration: under a minute
Perspective: Link, eyewitness

"This involved my father, a completely unreasonable individual. I don't associate with the man since he threw me down the basement stairs. Six foot, 220, ex-Marine, black belt in karate. A very bad mutherfucker. He fought 20 Mexicans at the Latino festival once—a big fucking Puerto Rican!

"We're driving up Light Street by the Inner Harbor when these two fucking whiteboys pulled up at the light and started talking shit. Big fucking muscleheads, but they're white. Like how many white guys can really fight? White guys can be cool, but who told 'em they could fight? Sure, some can. I had some friends in the Fourth Reich that were tough. But, in general, whiteboys should stick to wife-beating— that's what they're good at.

"These guys were getting out of their car, big mutherfuckers, and one of them [the passenger] had a pipe. We're on the right. Dad said, 'Stay here.' Then he got out, kicked the door shut on this guy, and beat the fuck out of him until the other guy got around. Then he drove a side kick into this fucker's chest and put him down.

"It was beautiful, baby. I was sitting there yelling, 'Go, Dad! Kick their fucking asses! Fuck 'em up!'

"A shame I didn't have any popcorn. He was standing over the guy he kicked, beating his ass. Then the other dude was getting up, so he went over and beat him back down into the ground.

"It was a beautiful night. The city was all lit up. I was jamming to some tunes on the radio and watching two exquisite ass kickings. Well, that man got back into the car, and we pulled off while they were crawling back into their car. They *thought* they were tough. Dad *knew* he was tough."

BRETT

Time of occurrence: day
Duration: seconds
Perspective: first-person aggressor

"I was working on a remodeling job when this older guy thought he was going to mess with me. I was using a cordless Makita 12-volt power drill with a half-inch chuck. It worked better as a weapon than as a tool. When he grabbed me, I head-butted him off me and swung. The steel housing opened up a cut on his head. Of course, we both got fired. I'd have to say I'm satisfied with the outcome."

EDWIN AND VIOLET

Time of occurrence: day
Duration: seconds
Perspective: first-person defender

"You know, it was another disagreement. I was standing out back here next to the fence. She pulled up in the van, pinned my leg between the fence and the bumper, and gave 'er a little gas. Tore all the ligaments. She took me to the hospital. It was an accident, of course."

Bobo's chair defense against the chucks.

RON'S VAN: A CAUTIONARY TALE

My roommate Ron, Darrin, and two biker chicks headed for Washington, D.C., one cold winter night to see a favorite band. On the way out of town, Ron picked up a female hitchhiker wearing *nothing* but tennis shoes, jeans, and a denim jacket. When the group arrived at the door of the nightclub, it was discovered that the hitchhiker had no ID or money, so the doormen refused to admit her. Worried that she would die of exposure in his unheated van, Ron was trying to talk the bouncers into letting her in when she suddenly stripped and started dancing for them. Assured that the girl's heavily tattooed body was indeed 21 years old, the bouncers admitted her free of charge.

On the way out of D.C., Ron [a racist] picked up a black man "shivering to death in a windbreaker," who was thumbing a ride to a local D.C. destination. By the time Ron got halfway up I-95 to Baltimore, the case of wine he had drunk that day [he was 6 feet, 6 inches and 350 pounds] finally took its toll, and he rolled the van, shattering the windshield. All six people, including the mystery stripper and the terrified black man, were unhurt. Ron and Darrin rolled the van back onto its wheels and continued to Baltimore.

Ron dropped the shivering, penniless black man off in a high-crime white neighborhood. While Ron was there, the police finally caught up to him and ticketed him for the windshield, and his regular girl was rudely introduced to his new possession in the dingy confines of his bedroom.

Dude, do not get in the biker's van.

CHAPTER THIRTEEN

ON THE DOWNSIDE OF LIFE

Living Peacefully Amid Predation

When I undertook this study, I sought to understand the nature of violent people. Except for being able to link certain behaviors with certain weapons, I have largely failed. I can, however, say this: violent men are painfully predictable—if we only bother to pay attention—and they are not violent often. All the violence engaged in by Duncan, Raphael, The Mac Daddy, and Tattoo Rick during the course of their relatively brutal lives would not fill one calendar day.

Most men of this type manage to carve out a nonviolent niche for themselves by the time they reach 30 and are generally no longer violent by age 50. Remember, though, that they reside in the gray areas of a society with which they are at odds on a primal level. The fact is, if you are polite you most likely will never become physically embroiled with someone of this type. They are like flytraps. They do not actively seek, but simply accept, the mayhem that others would reject. Where unarmed attacks and the use of blunt weapons are concerned, it is the aggressive group that is of more concern for those of us who want to live free of coercion.

While the individual who is willing to attack you with a blade usually acts as an individual, every other type of weapon tends to be used by members of aggressive groups. A weapon is not used simply to gain an advantage; it is often used maliciously by those who already have the advantage of numbers, surprise, or even size.

Pay attention and be careful.

CHAPTER FOURTEEN

BEATING THE ODDS

A Summary of Relevant Findings

The total number of incidents researched in this study (1,675) is strong, in that it represents triple the sample size usually deemed necessary for an accurate survey (500). However, these numbers may be skewed in ways that I do not understand, as I am not a statistician. Also, the smaller numbers may amplify some distortions.

First though, a little housekeeping. I need to define terminology used and weapon categories.

TERMINOLOGY

- *Acts* are violent situations.
- *All violence* is understood to be all 1,675 acts documented by the author.
- *Uses* are specific incidents of weapon usage. For example, when Link and his friends attacked the rival gang using two bats, that was one act but comprised two uses.
- *KO* indicates unconsciousness and/or incapacitation.
- *Legal* indicates that some form of civil or criminal action was at least initiated.

WEAPON CATEGORIES

- Edged weapon
- Firearms and chemical
- Club
- Common article or improvised weapon
- Stick
- Stone
- Tool
- Machinery and furniture

RESULTS

- Alcohol was involved in 525 of the 1,675 acts. Intoxication seems to make violence more likely and less serious, with the exception that the likelihood of death is identical. When alcohol is involved, the action is:
  —7 percent more likely to be a mutual
    combat as opposed to an attack
  —8 percent less likely to involve a weapon
  —4 percent more likely to result in a KO

- Grappling was common in the acts of violence.
  —41 percent of violent acts involve grappling.
  —33 percent of grappling encounters go to the floor.
  —14 percent of all violent acts go to the floor.

- Approximately 45 percent of the acts of violence resulted from unarmed attacks or blunt weapon aggression.
  —64 percent of injuries were to the head.
  —21 percent of injuries were to the torso.
  —15 percent of injuries were to the limbs.
  —54 percent of the encounters in this study were unarmed.

- Clubs account for 5 percent of the violent acts and 12 percent of the blunt-force encounters.

- Untrained individuals with sticks were just as successful as criminal groups with sticks, and law officers and stick fighters were both twice as likely to succeed as the untrained individual or criminal group.

- Stonings by groups were twice as likely to be successful as those by individuals. The only stonings resulting in death or legal actions were those committed by groups.

ABOUT THE AUTHOR

James LaFond lives, works, and writes in Baltimore, Maryland. He has somehow survived 21 boxing matches and 618 stick fights. If you would like to beat James with a stick, you may find contact information for him at www.jameslafond.com. For related articles, go to this website and click on Harm City.